Rape Culture, Purity Culture, and Coercive Control in Teen Girl Bibles

In this fascinating book, Caroline Blyth takes a close look at Bibles marketed to teen girls and asks how these might perpetuate harmful gender stereotypes that lie at the heart of rape culture.

The author considers the devotionals, commentaries, and advice sections placed throughout these Bibles, which offer teen girl readers life advice on topics such as friendships, body image, and how to navigate romantic relationships. Within these discussions, there is a strong emphasis on modesty, purity, and sexual passivity as markers of young women's 'godliness'. Yet, as the author argues, these gendered ideals are prescribed to readers using rape-supportive discourses and the tactics of coercive control. Moreover, the placement of these various editorial inserts within the pages of sacred scripture gives them considerable power to reinforce deeply harmful ideologies about gender, sexuality, and sexual violence. Given the seeming popularity of these Bibles among Christian teen girls, the need to dismantle their damaging rhetoric is especially urgent.

This book will be of particular interest to those studying the Bible, religion, gender, and theology, as well as the general reader.

Caroline Blyth is Senior Lecturer and Assistant Dean of Equity at the University of Auckland, New Zealand.

Rape Culture, Religion and the Bible
Series Editors:
Caroline Blyth
University of Auckland, New Zealand
Johanna Stiebert
University of Leeds, UK

Rape Myths, the Bible and #MeToo
Johanna Stiebert

Telling Terror in Judges 19
Rape and Reparation for the Levite's Wife
Helen Paynter

Resisting Rape Culture
The Hebrew Bible and Hong Kong Sex Workers
Nany Nan Hoon Tan

The Bible and Sexual Violence Against Men
Chris Greenough

Rape Culture, Purity Culture, and Coercive Control in Teen Girl Bibles
Caroline Blyth

For more information about this series, please visit: https://www.routledge.com/Rape-Culture-Religion-and-the-Bible/book-series/RCRB

Rape Culture, Purity Culture, and Coercive Control in Teen Girl Bibles

Caroline Blyth

LONDON AND NEW YORK

First published 2021
by Routledge
2 Park Square, Milton Park, Abingdon, Oxon OX14 4RN

and by Routledge
52 Vanderbilt Avenue, New York, NY 10017

Routledge is an imprint of the Taylor & Francis Group, an informa business

© 2021 Caroline Blyth

The right of Caroline Blyth to be identified as author of this work has been asserted by her in accordance with sections 77 and 78 of the Copyright, Designs and Patents Act 1988.

All rights reserved. No part of this book may be reprinted or reproduced or utilised in any form or by any electronic, mechanical, or other means, now known or hereafter invented, including photocopying and recording, or in any information storage or retrieval system, without permission in writing from the publishers.

Trademark notice: Product or corporate names may be trademarks or registered trademarks, and are used only for identification and explanation without intent to infringe.

British Library Cataloguing-in-Publication Data
A catalogue record for this book is available from the British Library

Library of Congress Cataloging-in-Publication Data
Names: Blyth, Caroline, 1967- author.
Title: Rape culture, purity culture, and coercive control in teen girl Bibles / Caroline Blyth.
Description: Abingdon, Oxon ; New York, NY : Routledge, 2021. | Series: Rape culture, religion and the bible | Includes bibliographical references and index. |
Identifiers: LCCN 2020043344 | ISBN 9780367245146 (hbk) | ISBN 9780429282959 (ebk)
Subjects: LCSH: Sex in the Bible. | Rape in the Bible. | Teenage girls--Conduct of life. | Teenage girls--Sexual behavior. | Teenage Girls--Religious aspects. | Bible--Criticism, interpretation, etc.
Classification: LCC BS680.S5 B59 2021 | DDC 220.8/3067--dc23
LC record available at https://lccn.loc.gov/2020043344

ISBN: 978-0-367-24514-6 (hbk)
ISBN: 978-0-429-28295-9 (ebk)

Typeset in Times New Roman
by MPS Limited, Dehradun

To all teen girls. Everywhere.

Contents

Acknowledgements   viii

Introduction   1

1 Purity, modesty, and rape culture in teen girl Bibles   10

2 Erasing rape in teen girl Bibles and contemporary culture   33

3 Christian complementarianism and coercive control in teen girl Bibles   68

Conclusion   97

Bibliography   99
Index of authors   105
Index of biblical citations   107

Acknowledgements

With thanks to Lily Van Buskirk and Julia Snodgrass, whose research assistance provided me with many valuable insights into the evangelical teen girl "industry" that I discuss in this book.

Special thanks to Olivia Stanley, whose own wonderful research into evangelical Christian purity culture has been a source of inspiration for me.

And a final thank you to Chris Greenough, who encouraged me to keep writing this book and got me through the days when I really didn't want to keep going with it.

Introduction

Since the late twentieth century, a number of publishers have marketed various "niche" versions of the Christian Bible to specific consumer groups, including men, women, parents, children, tweens, and teens (Nord 2004; cited in Moslener 2017, 621). These Bibles often supplement the biblical text with various editorial notes, devotionals, special features, and study guides, which speak to aspects of life and faith identified as pertinent to their market audience.

In this book, I explore one particular corner of this Bible industry: namely, Bibles produced for teenage girls, specifically girls around 13–17 years old who have graduated beyond the girl/tween age range. I focus my discussion on three of these Bibles, all of which are currently in print and therefore widely available: *Revolve* (Thomas Nelson 2012), *True Images* (Zondervan 2017), and the *Bible for Teen Girls* (Zondervan 2015). These three Bibles are created by and for the evangelical Christian community, which currently constitutes the single largest religious group in the United States, with over a quarter of Americans and a third of American teens identifying as members (Pew Research Center 2019a; Klein 2018, Introduction, Kindle).[1] This community is global, diverse, and fluid, crossing class, ethnic, and racial lines; in the United States alone, there are white, African-American, Hispanic, Asian-American, and mixed evangelical congregations.[2] Nevertheless, the majority of its US members are white, as well as culturally (if not politically) conservative.[3] Many evangelical groups also embrace traditional doctrines of gender and sexuality, which promote God-given "ideals" of (hetero)sexual purity, male authority, and female subordination (Moslener 2015, 2017; Klein 2018; Colgan 2018).

The three evangelical teen girl Bibles I study in this book include a range of editorial features that sit nestled within the biblical text; these features include profiles of biblical women, short devotionals, and life advice on topics such as friendships, family, school, pop culture, and romantic/sexual relationships.[4] Additionally, there is a great deal of pink font, pink paisley, love hearts, and flowers—"traditionally recognized images of femininity" that publishers use to sell these Bibles to their target audience (Moslener 2017, 610).

The editorial inserts in these three Bibles cover issues that are undoubtedly important for many teen girls. Yet, as I demonstrate throughout this book, these inserts are heavily encoded with troubling ideologies of gender and sexuality. Specifically, the notes, devotionals, and other features regularly promote the importance of girls' sexual purity and modesty; they also emphasize complementarian understandings of gender, which grant a divine mandate to male authority and female subordination (see Moslener 2017, 613–14). As such, these Bibles reinforce various evangelical discourses that scaffold rape cultures—cultures where sexual violence is normalized, ignored, and essentially allowed to flourish. These evangelical discourses measure a woman's social and spiritual worthiness according to her sexual status. They fetishize female virginity and chastity to the extent that rape victims are effectively rendered "damaged goods." They also re-inscribe the misperception, so common within rape cultures, that women's sexuality is naturally passive, while men are "hardwired" to be sexual aggressors. Women must therefore take responsibility for safeguarding their sexual chastity because men just "can't help themselves" when a woman "tempts" them sexually. This effectively shifts the culpability for rape from perpetrator to victim, while problematizing understandings of sexual consent.

These deeply patriarchal and rape-supportive discourses repeatedly recur within the three teen girl Bibles I look at in this book. There are literally *hundreds* of editorial inserts peppered throughout each Bible, positioned (quite literally) within the pages of sacred scripture. Located thus, their ideologically laden messages are imbued with spiritual authority, reifying their truth claims to teen girl readers and presenting them as eternally relevant and "inherently biblical" (Moslener 2017, 610; also Bennetch 2009, 44–49). Moreover, by including girls' names, pictures, and testimonies (real and fictional), these notes, devotionals, and profiles also attempt to relay a certain authenticity and contemporary relevance to readers, reminding them that every aspect of their lives is guided and prescribed by sacred scripture (see Kaell 2010).

Of course, not every teen girl who reads one of these Bibles will absorb its gendered ideologies unquestioningly (in other words, I should stop fretting). As Hilary Kaell's (2010) research suggests, readers may approach these editorial notes with a critical (or even sceptical) eye, challenging their claims about gender roles and "godly" teenage girls. At the same time, however, I have no doubt that some teen readers may feel pressured to accept these Bibles' teachings, particularly when their friends, family members, pastors, and youth group leaders are endorsing a similar worldview (see Stanley 2020). My concern, then, is that Bibles such as *True Images*, *Revolve*, and the *Bible for Teen Girls* could negatively impact teen girls' understandings of their own gendered identities and sexual selves. Kathryn Klement and Brad Sagarin note that "Adolescence is a period of life when individuals are constructing their identities; thus, messages received about sexuality and individual worth might be especially influential" (2017, 207).[5] But maybe that's the point. As Sarah Moslener notes, the evangelical movement views adolescence as "a precarious stage of development in which unformed psyches and moral codes are vulnerable against the adult urges brought on by puberty. For evangelicals, the transition from child to adult is especially precarious if an adolescent is not supported with proper spiritual guidance" (2015, Kindle Introduction).

Teen girl Bibles, with their relentless editorial notes, devotionals, and advice columns, are thus created by the evangelical community to provide such "spiritual guidance."[6] I contend, however, that the "guidance" they offer could do more harm than good. These Bibles prescribe strict regulations around female sexuality and purity, casting shame and stigma on any girl who fails to conform. They also misrepresent gender-based violence in a number of troubling ways, which could compromise the self-worth of teen girls victimized by such violence. The Bibles, therefore, have significant power, not only to shape what teen girls believe— about themselves, about the world, and about their faith—but also to police and manipulate their behaviour and their identities. As Edwin Black notes, rhetorical discourses can entice readers "not simply to believe something, but to *be* something" (1993, 172; emphasis original; cited in Bennetch 2009). And in the following chapters of this book, I argue that teen girl Bible readers are continually encouraged to *be* girls who passively accept subordination at the hands of male authority figures, who relinquish their sexual and social agency to male control, and who associate their sexuality and their bodies with shame, stigma, and sin. In other words, the teen girl Bibles discussed in this volume want to mould their readers into subordinated, shamed, policed, controlled, and silenced teenage girls.

Let me lay out how I tackle this issue in the rest of the book. In chapter 1, I begin my exploration of *True Images*, *Revolve*, and the *Bible for Teen Girls* by focusing on what these Bibles have to say about sexual purity and modesty. Studying their editorial notes in detail, I interrogate the ways that they reinforce evangelical purity discourse, which in turn sustains traditional gender stereotypes and rape-supportive ideologies. Through fetishizing virginity, these Bibles measure teen girls' moral and spiritual worth according to their sexual status, effectively shaming girls who choose to be sexually active and agentic. More than this, though, they also have the potential to stigmatize victims of sexual harm; their purity and modesty teachings inscribe shame on girls' bodies while shifting the blame for sexual aggression away from perpetrators and onto their victims.

In chapter 2, I consider the ways that sexual violence is spoken about (or not) in my three teen girl Bibles. I explore how these Bibles erase sexual violence in their profiles of biblical women and other editorial additions, by either ignoring it completely, reframing it as a sexual purity issue, or blaming the victims for their own assaults. I then consider these Bibles' troubling representations of sexual violence in contemporary contexts. Taken together, the three Bibles send a powerful message to teen girl readers: rape is either their fault, or it's not worth thinking about unless it threatens their sexual purity.

In the final chapter, I hone in on two of my teen girl Bibles (*True Images* and *Revolve*), mapping their perpetuation of harmful ideologies of gender and gendered violence. The notes, profiles, and devotionals included in *True Images* and *Revolve* reinforce complementarian discourses of female subordination by (unintentionally, perhaps) imitating tactics used by perpetrators of coercive control, including threats, degradation, isolation, microregulation, surveillance, love-bombing, and gaslighting. These Bibles' deluge of controlling rhetoric serves to intimidate readers into conforming to the evangelical ideal of teenage girlhood: obedient, subordinated, and silenced. It also sustains and normalizes religious and social discourses that make girls and women continually vulnerable to multiple forms of violence.

Before I draw this introduction to a close, let me offer some brief details about each of the three Bibles I scrutinize in the following chapters.

True Images

First published by Zondervan in 2003, the *True Images* Bible for teen girls has been reprinted and updated a number of times (2007, 2012, and 2017). Using the New International Version (NIV) translation, it supplements the biblical text with a great many editorial notes (one appears at least every couple of pages, and some pages contain multiple notes).

The introduction to *True Images* claims that:

> Every day, teen girls are bombarded with messages from the world about how they should look, act, think and talk. Another radio ad. Song lyrics. Air-brushed photos in a fashion magazine. Whether teens realize it or not, their minds are receiving those messages. But such messages "are all false! Their deeds amount to nothing; their images are but wind and confusion"
> (Isaiah 41:29). (ix)

The editorial voice of this Bible is deeply countercultural, and its notes, profiles, and devotionals repeatedly warn girls of the dangers of contemporary secular culture—including Hollywood movies, celebrity culture, music, make-up, and fashion magazines. It also regularly cites (out-of-context) Bible passages to articulate evangelical intolerance of bisexual, lesbian, and gay sexualities, transgender identities, non-Christian religions and religious pluralism, atheists, divorce, pre-marital sex, reproductive rights, and pro-choice advocacy.

The *True Images* introduction reassures readers that it offers a "truer" guide to "help teen girls make the connections between Scripture and life" (ix). It reminds them that God has a lot to say on the most important things in their lives: "friendships, future, family, dating, identity and image" (ix). The Bible, we are told, is "a manual for life," in which "God gives you the answers to your toughest questions" (ix).

This "manual," however, appears to require a great deal of editorial interference, including over a *thousand* notes, devotionals, and profiles added to its pages. There are 100 "In Focus" profiles—first-person accounts by (fictional) girls about their various life challenges, such as family and relationship troubles, bullying, anxiety, loneliness, and sexual temptations (the latter of which crops up a *lot*). The profiles offer readers an editorial evaluation/judgment of each girl's problem, as well as tips on how to deal with it, plus two or three biblical verses that lend a sense of scriptural validity to the advice given. Aside from these "In Focus" profiles, other features include 500 short "Dare to Believe" notes that give pithy reflections on specific biblical verses, and 300 "Genuine Notes" to help readers develop their "genuine" (i.e. spiritual) beauty and thus become a "beautiful girl" in God's eyes (ix). There are also page-long introductions to each biblical book and fifty-two "Mirror Images" profiles of the Bible's "leading ladies," who offer teen girls "both positive and negative role models" (x).[7] These "Mirror Images" profiles also "identify key personality traits and help you apply the lessons of these women's lives to your life today" (x). Each profile is accompanied by a simple pen-and-ink portrait (in pink!) of contemporary-looking teen girls, further inviting readers to associate themselves with the biblical women being profiled (Moslener 2017, 611).

The strangest additions to *True Images* are the 100 "Love Notes" from God, which are placed at regular intervals throughout its pages. These notes (pink again, with love hearts) are drawn to look like an actual note that someone has left inside this Bible. Written in a Comic Sans-style font that emulates neat handwriting, each note is addressed to the reader with some endearment or other ("Daughter," "Loved One," "My child," etc.), and is signed by God himself in a curlier, cursive font ("Your Father," "Father God," or "Dad"). I must confess I found these notes quite disturbing—they felt so intrusive, as though someone had gone through my Bible when I wasn't looking and left me unsolicited declarations of love. I discuss the equally disquieting content of these notes later in Chapter 3.

Lastly, *True Images* includes six eight-page colour inserts, all of which are printed on glossy paper and emulate the style of a teen girl fashion magazine. These inserts cover a range of topics (e.g. friendship, self-confidence, spiritual gifts, and guys), using lifestyle quizzes and advice columns to impart their wisdom. Photos of brightly smiling teenage girls add a touch of authenticity, inviting readers to see the personal relevance of the material presented on these pages. The girls always look happy and healthy, with shiny hair and perfect skin and teeth; they are also always attractive, able-bodied, and slim, reinforcing Western beauty ideals of "perfect" femininity.

Revolve

Revolve is published by Thomas Nelson, and of the three Bibles I looked at, it is by far the prettiest.[8] My copy has a faux-leather cover in bright fuchsia, with painted and embossed flowers front and back (and even more flowers printed on the pages' fore-edge in a lovely turquoise shade). There is plenty of pink inside as well (contrasted nicely with chocolate brown detail),[9] and paisley patterns abound. The biblical text used in this Bible is the New Century Version (NCV), which the Bible's Preface claims is both "trustworthy" and "clear" (xii).

Revolve's editorial additions follow a similar style to *True Images*, including 365 devotional notes (called "Daily Devos"), biblical book introductions ("The Big Picture"), and six glossy magazine-style inserts packed with quizzes, Bible study notes, photos of grinning teen girls, and advice columns. There are also profiles of biblical women

("Ladies of the Bible") which, akin to *True Images*, ask readers to compare themselves (favourably or unfavourably) with these characters. The profiles are written in an interesting narrative style (as though the biblical text was being novelized), and much artistic licence is used to present these biblical women's thoughts and emotions, rendering them more relatable to readers.

All of the inserts, profiles, and "Daily Devos" in *Revolve* use the biblical texts to reflect on issues that editors believe affect teen girls' lives, including loneliness, relationship troubles, and (of course) sexual purity. The same presumption is made here as we find in *True Images*: girls must learn to see the myriad connections and resonances between the Bible and their lives because this book is their daily guide. And, like *True Images*, this Bible is fairly suspicious of contemporary popular culture; girls are therefore regularly cautioned to approach it with care.

The Bible for Teen Girls

Like *True Images*, the *Bible for Teen Girls* (2015) is published by Zondervan and uses the NIV translation. Just as pink as the other two Bibles, it includes an introduction to each biblical book, and peppers the biblical text with over 250 devotionals (titled "Growing in Faith, Hope, Love") and fifty profiles of biblical women ("Women of the Bible"). Some of these page-long devotionals have been authored by the Bible's editors, but many are excerpts from other books published by Zondervan, including Christian self-help literature and inspiring stories written by evangelical Christian women. This Bible, therefore, also serves as an advertisement for other Zondervan products.

The editorial intrusions in the *Bible for Teen Girls* are a bit more low-key than in *Revolve* and *True Images*. All the devotionals and profiles take up an entire page, rather than being split into innumerable nifty text boxes, so their frequency feels less unremitting, and the evangelical rhetoric is less persistent. The blurb on the back cover tells readers that this Bible is "designed for real teen girls with real lives," and offers readers "promises of God, challenging insights, smart advice, and open discussions about the realities of life." Like the other two Bibles, then, this is marketed as a text that is relevant to teen girls' lives and experiences. The devotionals draw on biblical passages to reflect on day-to-day issues that girls may encounter, including relationship conflicts, crises of faith, and the temptations of the contemporary world (including sexual temptations, of course).

Two final things to keep in mind

Throughout this book, I include a lot of quotes from the various editorial inserts (notes, profiles, and devotionals) in my three teen girl Bibles. Each of these inserts is located on one page only; that is, they never span across two or more pages. So, when I first mention or quote from a particular insert, I give the page number in an in-text citation but do not repeat this if I quote/mention it again in subsequent sentences within the same paragraph. This is to save some of my paragraphs being peppered by heaps of in-text citations. I'm fairly confident you won't get confused. And to be extra clear about which of the three Bible I am quoting from, I include an abbreviation of the title along with the page numbers: *TIB* for *True Images* Bible; *RB* for *Revolve* Bible; and *BTG* for the *Bible for Teen Girls*. So, to give an example, an in-text citation that reads (*RB* 230) lets you know that the editorial note I am discussing is on p. 230 of *Revolve*.

A final note and word of caution. When I first told a friend that I was writing a book about teen girl Bibles, she laughed and said, "That sounds like fun!" But to be honest, it wasn't fun at all. Reading three evangelical teen girl Bibles from cover to cover proved exhausting, depressing, and demoralizing. Because whether they mean to or not, these Bibles repeatedly question teen girls' right to any sense of sexual agency. They shame girls for having an embodied presence in the world. They give voice to various myths and ideologies that allow rape cultures to flourish. They employ the rhetorical tactics of coercive control to bury their readers in helplessness and shame. And they normalize harmful gender stereotypes that scaffold patriarchal privilege, subordinate women and girls, and minimize the severity of gender-based violence.

Continue this book with care, dear readers, and don't let these Bibles get you down.

Notes

1 The evangelical Christian movement arose in the mid-twentieth century and has quickly become a hugely significant part of the US religious landscape. See Fitzgerald (2017) and Moslener (2015) for more on the history of American evangelicalism.
2 According to Pew Research Center (2019c) statistics, 78 per cent of US evangelical Protestant Christians are white, 11 per cent are Hispanic, 6 per cent are Black, 2 per cent are Asian, and the remaining 5 per cent are "mixed."
3 The Pew Research Center (2019a, 2019b) notes that 55 per cent of evangelical Christians identify as being politically "conservative."

Introduction 9

4 I am unable to share an image of these Bibles for copyright reasons, but to see what a typical page looks like, the two Zondervan Bibles can be viewed at https://www.amazon.com/True-Images-Bible-Leathersoft-Blue/dp/0310080045/ref=sr_1_1?dchild=1&keywords=true+images+bible&qid=1605921027&sr=8-1, and a slightly earlier version of the *Revolve* Bible is viewable here http://everylittlething.squarespace.com/revolve-bible-10/ (the cartoon pictures in this version have been replaced by photographs of teen girls in the edition that I have, but the text appears unchanged).

5 See also Allen (2005, 2011, 2013) for further discussion of factors influencing the development of adolescent girls' sexual identities and sexual selves, particularly in terms of their schooling and education.

6 Of course, Bibles are not the only means by which the evangelical movement attempts to "guide" teenage girls (and guys); a plethora of other products are marketed, including teen girl devotionals, self-help books and guides, websites, YouTube channels, DVDs, and other educational materials. I mention some of these in the coming chapters but do not have the space to explore them all in depth. That would require another (at least one) Routledge Focus volume.

7 Both *True Images* and *Revolve* include profiles of biblical "bad girls"—such as Eve, Delilah, Jezebel—whom teen girls are warned *not* to emulate (see *TIB*, 5, 482, 865; *RB* 5, 293, 434). And while the sins of Eve, Delilah, and Jezebel are not always framed in an explicitly sexualized light, these profiles continue to peddle the same tired stereotypes of woman as "temptress" and a source of sin (Moslener 2017, 611).

8 Thomas Nelson published an earlier iteration of *Revolve*, titled *Revolve: The Complete New Testament* (2003). Designed to look like a teen girl fashion magazine, the pages of this Biblezine brim with endless photos, profiles, Q&A columns, (spiritual) beauty tips, dating advice, diary features, and other reflections on teen girls' lives and faith. *Revolve: The Complete New Testament* was hugely successful when it was first launched, selling over 40,000 copies in the first month, and well over half a million copies up to the present time. Fascinating as I find this Biblezine, I (reluctantly) chose not to discuss it in this book because it appears to be out of print (I only managed to get hold of a second-hand copy by tracking one down online). But to learn more about it and its later editions (which are likewise not currently in print), see Moslener (2017); Bennetch (2009); Kaell (2010). And if you manage to get hold of one, it's definitely worth a look.

9 My favourite chocolate in a selection box used to be raspberry or strawberry crème. But after trawling through *Revolve*, with its endless pink and chocolate brown colourscape, I swear I'll never be able to stomach one again.

1 Purity, modesty, and rape culture in teen girl Bibles

In this chapter, I consider the ways that evangelical teen girl Bibles reinforce a discourse of purity, which in turn sustains traditional gender stereotypes and rape-supportive ideologies. The purity discourse is centred on the belief that girls' and women's social "value" is contingent on their virginity/chastity and their ability to remain sexually "pure." Rooted in patriarchal gender ideals, it fetishizes virginity (Valenti 2009, 14) and carries the expectation that "girls and women, in particular, will be utterly and absolutely nonsexual until the day they marry a man" (Klein 2018, ch. 3, Kindle; also Klement and Sagarin 2017, 208). This purity discourse is not only found in religious ideology, but reflects wider socio-cultural beliefs about gender, female sexuality, and women's moral currency. As Jessica Valenti argues, "Idolizing virginity as a stand-in for women's morality means that nothing else matters—not what we accomplish, not what we think, not what we care about and work for. Just if/how/whom we have sex with. That's all" (2009, 24). Moreover, the purity discourse tightly connects women's ethical identity to their body in a way that celebrates their passivity, suggesting that "women can't be moral actors. Instead, we're defined by what we don't do—our ethics are the ethics of passivity" (Valenti 2009, 25).

Despite being endorsed by both religious and secular communities, the sexual purity discourse has been the "most stubborn message" of evangelical church teachings for decades, rising to especial prominence since the late 1980s and 1990s (Stanley 2020, 119).[1] Following wider evangelical trends of using certain popular culture formats to disseminate their doctrines, teachings on sexual purity are sold to evangelical Christian tweens, teens, and young adults (as well as their parents) through purity industry products, including highly editorialized Bibles, popular books, magazines, and devotionals,[2] DVDs, blogs, vlogs, Bible study programmes, seminars, purity balls,[3] abstinence-only sex education programmes,[4] and a plethora of other commodities including purity rings,[5] bracelets, necklaces, mugs, and T-shirts (Klein 2018, Introduction, Kindle). Evangelical groups such as Silver Ring Thing and True Love Waits run events and offer products that continually stress the connection between purity and faith, making the latter unequivocally contingent on the former. In the United States alone, these groups have reached millions of young people (Moslener 2017, 609). Their events and products essentially sell sexual purity to young evangelicals as the sole option available to them: they reinforce the evangelical belief that sexual abstinence before marriage is the only way to live as a Christian and that any form of premarital sexual activity is a threat to one's physical, emotional, and spiritual health (Moslener 2015, Introduction, Kindle). The only "safe sex" before marriage is no sex at all.

Although these purity industry products are marketed to both male and female evangelicals, their messaging and modes of delivery are highly encoded for gender—fetishizing and commodifying female chastity as part of the natural, divinely created order. As I discuss in this chapter, the contemporary evangelical purity industry repackages traditional gender norms that frame male sexuality as actively aggressive and female sexuality as passive and shameful, and naturally so. God, it appears, designed men to be "hardwired" to search out sex; women are therefore tasked with protecting their purity from male sexual advances, all the while suppressing or denying their own (sinful and dangerous) sexuality and sexual desires. Female tweens, teens, and young women are taught that their "sexual thoughts, feelings, and choices determine [their] spiritual standing" (Klein 2018, Introduction, Kindle), and therefore have the potential to be a source of sin and defilement, not only for themselves but also for the men they encounter. Men, meanwhile, can be secretly proud of their own voracious sexual appetites, safe in the knowledge that these are natural and God-given.

To be honest, the contemporary evangelical purity movement of the twentieth and twenty-first centuries is not saying anything terribly new; sexual chastity is a mainstay of most conservative religious communities. What is new, however, is the way that it has framed sexual chastity as a public and political form of religious testimony, rather than a private and personal choice (Moslener 2015, Introduction, Kindle). Drawing on the rhetoric of moral panic and apocalyptic anxiety, the evangelical purity discourse pushes back against what evangelicals perceive to be the widespread cultural degeneration of sexual morality, which began during the "sexual revolution" of the 1960s and has led to our current "sex-saturated" culture (Moslener 2015, Introduction, Kindle). Young people's ability to preserve their sexual integrity is viewed as an almost impossible task, "given the temptations of internal sexual urges and an external culture that teases young people with the titillations of sexual experimentation" (Moslener 2015, Introduction, Kindle). Appealing to discourses of public health and therapeutic spirituality, evangelical sexual purity rhetoric is therefore presented as a vital part of adolescents' spiritual, mental, and physical wellbeing (Moslener 2015, Introduction, Kindle; Williams 2011, 430–34). And even when scientific studies demonstrate that abstinence-only sex education programmes are ineffective and may compromise adolescent wellbeing,[6] proponents of the evangelical purity discourse draw instead on theological and biblical rationales to justify their teachings. Outward, embodied choices (such as abstinence) become evidence of one's godly soul—an external marker of one's spiritual health and commitment to the evangelical God.

As I noted at the start of this chapter, the evangelical Christian church is not the only voice perpetuating this highly gendered purity discourse; many of the same ideologies underpinning it—"natural" female sexual passivity and male sexual aggression, the shaming of female sexuality, and the sexualized woman as morally "damaged goods"—are equally dominant in wider contemporary culture. But the evangelical community does have a particularly prominent and powerful voice in this discussion, especially given the community's global reach and the way that its teachings embed purity messaging within religious dogma and biblical authority. It's so much harder to debate these ideations of purity when your salvation is on the line.

Yet it is a debate worth fighting over. The purity rhetoric expressed in the teen girl Bibles I examine prioritizes young women's purity and modesty as markers of their "godly" character. At the heart of this rhetoric, however, is a desire to control girls' and women's bodies and to erase sexual violence as a serious social concern (Klement and Sagarin 2017). Purity products aimed at evangelical teen girls reinforce discourses of sexuality and gender that lie at the heart of rape culture: discourses that measure a woman's social and spiritual worth according to her sexual status, particularly her chastity, and that put the onus of responsibility onto women for guarding their chastity and negotiating consent (or more importantly, *withholding* consent). These discourses help to perpetuate the myths that a rape victim is "damaged goods" as the result of losing her chastity or "purity," and that she was likely to blame for her assault because she "tempted" her attacker with her immodest appearance or behaviour (her "lack" of purity, as it were). They also re-inscribe the misperception, so common in rape cultures, that women must take responsibility for safeguarding their sexual chastity because men "just can't help themselves" when it comes to matters of sex. This, once again, effectively shifts the culpability for rape from perpetrator to victim, while problematizing understandings of sexual violence and consent (Kramer and Sagarin 2017). As Olivia Stanley observes, "The rhetoric of man's uncontrollable lust seems an odd bedfellow for purity discourses, yet they lie hand in hand" (2020, 119). Or, in the words of Valenti, "So long as women are supposed to be 'pure', and so long as our morality is defined by our sexuality, sexualized violence against us will continue to be both accepted and expected" (2009, 147; see also Anne 2012).

Moreover, purity culture messaging also has the potential to undermine the mental health and wellbeing of evangelical women and girls who remain its chief targets. According to Linda Kay Klein (a former member of an evangelical community which endorsed purity culture teachings):

> Evangelical Christianity's sexual purity movement is traumatizing many girls and maturing women haunted by sexual and gender-based anxiety, fear, and physical experiences that sometimes mimic the symptoms of post-traumatic stress disorder (PTSD). Based on our nightmares, panic attacks, and paranoia, one might think that my childhood friends and I had been to war. And in fact, we had. We went to war with ourselves, our own bodies, and our own sexual natures, all under the strict commandment of the church.
>
> (2018, Introduction, Kindle)

Klein describes feeling a sense of shame about her own sexualized body as she grew up, which manifested later in her adult relationships.[7] Her teenage encounter with evangelical purity culture left her carrying the shame, fear, and anxiety of being "impure"—a "stumbling block" and source of temptation for men (2018, Introduction, Kindle). She was taught that sexual purity was an external marker of a person's worthiness to belong to the evangelical community; sex was a measure of how close a person was to God, how "true" a Christian they were. But as Klein notes, "The [evangelical] purity message is not about sex. Rather, it is about *us*: who we are, who we are expected to be, and who it is said we will become if we fail to meet those expectations. This is the language of shame" (2018, Introduction, Kindle; emphasis original). The evangelical purity movement thus embeds shame in girls and young women about who they are as social, spiritual, and sexual subjects. This shame is "coiled around core beliefs, laced through theology, and twisted into doctrine, making it nearly impossible to see" or to challenge (Klein 2018, Introduction, Kindle). Moreover, such shame can lead girls and women who are victims of sexual violence to feel powerless, worthless, stigmatized, and blamed. As Valenti argues, the myth of sexual purity does far more harm to women than our "sex-saturated" culture ever could (2009, 9).

Just as the evangelical purity discourse is heavily encoded for gender, it also draws on malignant ideologies of race, class, and sexuality. In a church predominated by whiteness, and founded on white privilege (Moslener 2015, Introduction, Kindle), notions of female "purity" have always served to uphold the feminine "ideal" as white, middle-class, and heterosexual. Failing to fit into this ideal, women of colour, working-class women, and queer women therefore fail the purity test from the outset and are elided from most conversations about desirable femininity and sexuality (Collins 2000, 123–48). As Valenti observes, "How can you be 'pure' if you are seen as dirty to begin with? … Women of color, low-income women, immigrant women—these are the women who are not seen as worthy of being placed on a pedestal. It's only our perfect virgins who are valuable, worthy of discourse and worship" (2009, 45).

For the remainder of this chapter, I explore the ways that the three Bibles under discussion (*True Images*, *Revolve*, and the *Bible for Teen Girls*) target their "perfect virgin" teen girl audience with purity messaging. Drawing on examples from these Bibles, I contend that the purity discourse articulated therein serves to control and erase teen girls' sexuality, all the while reinforcing and perpetuating various rape myths and rape-supportive ideologies that scaffold rape cultures.

Keeping vertical on the slippery slope: the evangelical purity discourse

When virginity is fetishized, sex becomes taboo and shameful—something that should remain hidden and unspoken. Evangelical girls and women are thus taught that talking or thinking about sex, let alone enacting it, is a source of shame and sin (Klein 2018, ch. 3, Kindle). And through this miasma of silence around sex, teen girls must learn to navigate multiple prescriptions and proscriptions intended to keep them "pure." Definitions of "sex" and "sexual activity" are not typically restricted to penetrative sexual intercourse, but may include oral sex and masturbation (either mutual or solo).[8] Some evangelical teen Bibles and literature also urge caution with premarital kissing, petting, touching, sexting, lying down,[9] and even *thinking* about sex or having a crush, as well as watching sexual scenes or imagery in mainstream cinema, music videos, and *any* form of pornography.[10] As one *True*

Images "In Focus" profile insists, "Any activity that arouses sexual feelings is off-limits" to a girl until she is married (*TIB* 377). For these activities may lead her onto the slippery slope of sexual desire, and before you know it, she'll be sliding and slipping towards all manner of sexual impurity. The only sexual status that teen girls must hold onto is an *a*sexual status—they must remain virgins until they marry their first and only husband. Nothing else will do.

This emphasis on virginity is reinforced time and again throughout the teen girl Bibles I looked at, both explicitly in the didactic editorial notes and more implicitly too. For example, some of the "Mirror Images" profiles in *True Images* feature godly biblical women who are praised (among other things) for their chastity: the virgin-until-marriage Rebekah, who had a "servant's heart" (*TIB* 88), and (of course) the Virgin Mary, who is lauded particularly for "[keeping] herself pure in anticipation of her wedding night ... Mary knew she was on track with God and her man" (*TIB* 903). *True Images* readers are invited to emulate these biblical role-models, whose sexual purity has never been in doubt.

Yet, within the teen girl Bibles, one can detect a palpable fear that girls are always an inch away from losing their purity, often because they live in a "sex-saturated" culture. Editorial notes regularly warn readers against the dangers of various fleshly temptations wrought by a culture that does not take sex seriously enough. Girls must therefore be prepared to resist all the temptations that are thrown their way, from watching steamy love scenes in movies to having crushes on guys. In one *Bible for Teen Girls* devotional (an excerpt from Bekah Hamrick Martin's book, *The Bare Naked Truth*, published in 2013), readers are warned that "we're so saturated in our sex-crazed culture that our senses are numbed. Things we might have questioned before now don't even register. And if we're not prepared—if we haven't decided what to do in a tempting situation beforehand—we might as well just kiss our ideals good-bye" (*BTG* 1506). Sexual abstinence is heavily promoted, and a few pages later, another excerpt from Martin's (2013) book tells girls to "Run. Get away. Don't put yourself in a position to decide whether you need to use a condom. Don't get alone with a guy you find attractive" (*BTG* 1519). This, Martin insists, is "really the best form of birth control." Similarly, a *Revolve* "Daily Devos" note reminds girls that "God created sex for marriage alone. If you're in a relationship where you're having sex or toying with the idea, get out! Even if you're not in a relationship that has progressed to this point, be careful. Guard your thoughts and impulses ... Sexual sin is powerful and tricky" (*RB* 1387).

Evangelical teen girls must therefore police their own behaviour carefully, because if they don't, the repercussions are inevitably dire.

"Sex is never casual," they are advised (*TIB* 883), nor should it ever be shared with anyone other than the man they marry for life. Premarital sex is likened to "spilling your most valuable possession in the streets. It's like letting strangers splash in your most priceless fountain ... It isn't a recreational activity with someone who wanders into your life and tries to lead you astray. It isn't a gulp of water you grab wherever you can" (*BTG* 785). Sexual behaviour is never, ever "a fun activity for friends" (*TIB* 123) or "harmless fun" (*TIB* 543)—it is *always* dangerous and *always* damaging. "Love is like fire," *True Images* readers are warned, "once it's started, it's hard to put out. If you don't feel ready for a lifelong commitment, why play with fire? You will get badly burned" (*TIB* 1430). Yikes.

Time and again, then, these teen girl Bibles use editorial notes to persuade readers that God calls them to purity in order to "protect [them] from the dangers of misusing [their] sexuality" (*TIB* 233). Premarital sex and danger are frequently placed hand in hand, with girls receiving regular warnings that outside of marriage, sexual activity leads to a lifetime of misery, disease, shame, and sin. Horror stories of teen pregnancy and sexually transmitted infections abound in teen girl purity literature, and these teen girl Bibles are no exception.[11] A *Revolve* "Daily Devos" note on Song of Songs 4:12 (titled "Lock Up Your Garden, Girl!" *RB* 787) warns girls that having premarital sex "is like playing Russian roulette with STDs" and that "sleeping around cheapens the beauty of intimacy and leads to severe emotional damage." It is also "cruel," "emotionally devastating," results in "pain, fear, and distrust," and will "damage you emotionally and dishonour God's good plan for your life." In a similar vein, a *True Images* "Dare to Believe" note nestled next to Genesis 4 reminds readers that marriage is the only place for sex: "Did you know that God created sex ... as a gift for people? He also created the only safe place to open this gift—a committed marriage. All other places lead to disappointment and pain" (*TIB* 7).

Rather than offering advice about negotiating consent, effective birth control, safer sex, or healthy sexual relationships, these Bibles' various editorial notes regularly conflate sex and danger as a means of controlling teen girls' bodies and securing their conformity to the evangelical purity ideal (Stanley 2020). Any hint of girls' sexual agency is equated with their moral, spiritual, emotional, *and* physical destitution. Any promise of sexual pleasure is replaced by threats of shame, pain, and disease. The message is clear: teen girls and young women do not—*cannot*—know what is in their best interests or be trusted to take responsibility for their own sexual and social choices (Valenti 2009, 185–90). They must therefore relinquish their sexuality and their sexual autonomy if they wish to remain "pure" enough to be pleasing to God—*and* their future husband. The conflation of impurity with danger is therefore a powerful way to hegemonize teen girls' behaviour, reinforcing the belief that girls' social and spiritual value is contingent on the "purity" of their sexuality and their bodies, and that their bodies hold the ever-present potential to be a site of sin and (male) temptation (Klein 2018, ch. 3, Kindle). To lose one's purity is to lose one's right to belong in the evangelical faith community, not to mention one's access to God. For the deity constructed by evangelical Christianity has no tolerance of "impure" girls and women—sexualized teen girls' bodies will *always* provoke divine displeasure and disappointment.

This obsession with girls' and women's purity is, at its heart, heavily encoded for gender, and serves to reinforce traditional stereotypes about men and women. If teen girls are allowed to aspire to anything in these Bibles, it is to embrace a life of marriage and motherhood—in that order, of course. Readers are reminded on more than one occasion that a woman's sexuality, and her body, belong to men—first her father, then her husband, and *always* God; women cannot enjoy any sexual agency or sexual pleasure from their own bodies (Kramer and Sagarin 2017, 213). Nor can they be agentic or proactive in searching for "Mr Right," as God and God alone will decide if and when a girl can get married (I return to this in Chapter 3).

Once a teen girl grows up and gets married, her obedience, commitment, and subordination are shared between the deity and her husband. This message is reiterated throughout the *True Images* Bible. In the "Mirror Images" profile on Ruth, for example, girls are told not to worry about finding a boyfriend, but to "stay focused on [their] relationship with Jesus with all [their] might" until God decides to surprise them with a suitably godly guy (*TIB* 319). The readers' prayer that accompanies this profile says, "Dear God, show me how to fall in love with you first, so I'll know how to *care for the guy of my dreams*" (emphasis added). Clearly a girl just wants a husband so that she can spend all her time looking after him. And equally clearly, she is meant to love, obey, and serve him, just as she would her God.

Prayers for a life of wifely subordination continue in the *True Image*s introductory notes for Song of Songs, where girls are told, "Pray that if God has marriage in his plans for you, that you will be a loving and refreshing *part* of your husband's life" (*TIB* 874; emphasis added). And a "Dare to Believe" note reminds girls that "You can't give sex to get love. That never works! God intended your virginity to be an amazing *gift for your husband*" (*TIB* 879; emphasis added).

A girl's virginity is a commodity, it appears, to be passed from deity to husband, a fact reiterated in the "In Focus" profile about the value of virginity, which reminds girls again that "your virginity is a precious gift God gave you to *hand to your husband someday*" (*TIB* 883; emphasis added). Meanwhile, an "In Focus" profile about the dangers of oral sex (*TIB* 123) features a fictional girl called Ashley, who shakily tells readers that "my body belongs to [God] first and then to the man I will marry. If I share a few body parts with friends for recreation along the way, I'll be giving away my purity, little by little. Will I be losing myself along the way too?" No, Ashley, believe me, you won't.

Chewed gum: "damaged goods" and the purity discourse

Ashley's disembodied anxiety about becoming less than perfectly pure is a reminder that the sexual purity discourse frames premarital sexual behaviour of *any* sort as a source of girls' impurity. Purity is envisioned as a binary not a spectrum, especially for women and girls—there simply are no grey areas; if you aren't wholly pure (i.e. a virgin or chaste wife), you are by default *im*pure (i.e. a whore), and the consequences are dire. Girls who end up on the wrong side of the purity binary are, in evangelical eyes, a source of untold sin and shame, not to mention a dangerous source of defilement to godly guys who fall under their thrall (Klein 2018, ch. 3, Kindle). Girls and women who have sex are deemed "used" or damaged goods—a trashable "styrofoam cup" rather than a piece of priceless porcelain (Gresh 2012, ch. 8, Kindle). Sexual purity and abstinence teachings frequently use a range of object lessons to drive home a message that girls who have sex before marriage are spoiled, dirty, diseased, and lacking in moral and spiritual value. They are likened to chewed gum, sucked candy, licked and dirt-encrusted Oreo cookies, used handkerchiefs, pranged cars, and sticky tape covered in dust balls (see Klein 2018, Introduction, Kindle; Valenti 2009, 32–33). Klein notes with interest how many of these abstinence lessons are aimed specifically at girls, rather than both genders, and that they often involve food, as though girls are something to be consumed by men, and must therefore remain "palatable" lest they ruin the appetite of their future spouse or even make him barf (2018, Introduction, Kindle).

The teen girl Bibles I studied also perpetuate this image of the sexual girl as sullied or defiled. *True Images*, for example, includes a profile of Avery, who laments that she is "no longer a virgin" (*TIB* 1430). Avery feels the need to "admit" this because she has "felt awful" since she had sex with her boyfriend; she realized too late that it was "the biggest mistake" of her life as it has damaged her relationship with God. She now worries that she "messed up forever" and will never get back "what I gave away," as though she is now less of a person (echoing Ashley above). The advice offered after Avery's story reassures girls that if they lose their virginity, they can still regain their "sexual purity" through asking for "forgiveness"; God will forgive their sin (the sin of having sex), just as Jesus forgave the woman who was caught in adultery (John 8:2–11). The *Bible for Teen Girls* likewise uses this same biblical text to compare the woman caught in adultery with girls who commit "sexual sin" (*BTG* 1326). Girls are told to "pursue a life of purity. Keep yourself pure for the day you marry your husband." Both of these profiles frame teen girls who lose their virginity as sinners—akin to an adulteress about to face death by stoning. And while redemption and re-purification are possible, girls must first admit the shame of their sexuality and of their futile attempts at sexual agency.

The profile featuring Avery is fairly standard in evangelical Bibles, devotionals, and other books aimed at teen girls. Girls' virginity is fetishized, and its "loss" is mourned as a source of their remorse, unhappiness, and sin. As I mentioned at the start of the chapter, evangelical purity teachings often draw on the rhetoric of medical and public health warnings in order to claim some veracity and respectability. Thus, stories abound about girls who have sex outside of marriage and end up in a puddle of heartbreak and regret. Dannah Gresh's book, *And the Bride Wore White* (2012) is a "perfect" example of this. Essentially a long, threatening love letter to girls who may be tempted to forego their chastity, Gresh lays out with a terrifying relish a series of grim physical and psychological traumas caused by premarital sex. Her book (and others similar to it, e.g. Etheridge and Arterburn 2004) maps out the emotional and physical health risks of any form of sex (including unwanted pregnancies, sexually transmitted disease, cancer, depression, anxiety, and suicide), sometimes using highly debatable statistics to amplify these risks.[12] As Moslener notes, "In this way, religious ideologies impacting adolescent sexuality enter into the public sphere under the guise of mental health or therapeutic discourses, giving them credibility beyond their initial religious context" (2015, Introduction, Kindle). Drawing on patriarchal stereotypes, these ideologies reinforce the idea that a woman's worth is dependent on her sexual chastity or virginity, thereby stigmatizing, shaming, devaluing, and terrifying women who *choose* to be agentic and in control of their sexuality.

More than that though, and as Klement and Sagarin (2017, 219) note, this discourse of sex and impurity also does serious harm to women and girls who experience sexual harm. For many victims, their assault already leaves them with an overwhelming sense of having been defiled or degraded, as though the perpetrator has somehow sullied both their body and their mind. According to Leslie Lebotwitz and Susan Roth, sexual violence is a "powerful" form of interpersonal communication, whereby perpetrators make victims feel like a worthless object of abuse and contempt (1994, 366, 369–76).

Yet this message is also reinforced by common social responses; victims of sexual harm are often judged by their communities, cultures, or even their families and friends as having been damaged, devalued, and defiled as the result of their assault. This discourse of the rape victim as "damaged goods" is common currency in many societies and cultures spanning space and time. It is rooted in patriarchal gender norms, mentioned already in this chapter, which assign women a "value" based on their sexual chastity and "purity" (Brownmiller 1993, 376; also Blyth 2010, 98–99). Women's sexuality has long been viewed as a piece of sexual "property" owned by men (first their father, then their husband). Within this sexual economy, female sexuality is binarized into pure/impure or chaste/unchaste. When a woman remains the sole sexual property of her current "owner," she maintains her status as "chaste" and "pure." But once a woman crosses over the line from one binary category to the other (by having sexual contact with a man other than her rightful "owner"), she may be regarded as defiled and degraded, having lost her sexual and social value (Lebowitz and Roth 1994, 371–76).

Unfortunately, this ideology remains just as true for women and girls whose chastity and purity are deemed to have been "damaged" by sexual assault. Despite victims' lack of consent and the perpetrator's use of coercion and violence, the outcome remains the same, as though a woman's (albeit non-consensual) encounter with forbidden sexuality renders her no longer "pure"—polluted with the immorality of pre-marital or extramarital sex. Stigmatized and shamed by both her attacker *and* her community, her own sense of shame and defilement is thus twice confirmed. Some victims therefore decide not to report their assault, preferring to keep silent than face the shame and opprobrium that they know will be forthcoming. Sexual assault remains one of the most underreported crimes across the globe, and given the trauma many victims face after making a disclosure, this is not terribly surprising. Victims may know too well that they will be stained by ideologies of defilement and dishonour, socially ostracized, devalued, or even harmed by their family and community. So, they choose to say nothing, effectively silenced by a culture that insists on measuring women's moral value according to their sexual purity. As Klein argues, "purity culture excuses male sexuality and amplifies female sexuality, and it shames consensual sexual activity and silences nonconsensual sexual activity" (2019, ch. 13, Kindle).

This myth around women's sexual "value" lies at the heart of the purity discourse evoked in evangelical teen girl Bibles. And while the Bibles I studied for this volume respond to rape and sexual assault with some degree of sympathy (more of which later), their pervasive insistence on pushing purity as a sign of girls' moral and spiritual value is deeply unhelpful. Moreover, there is no statement made (explicitly or implicitly) about sexual violence *not* having an impact on a woman's purity; there is no reassurance that coercive and non-consensual sexual acts do *not* render women dirty, sinful, shamed, or defiled. When virginity and sexual purity are prioritized and fetishized to such a degree, then girls who fear they have lost their "purity" due to a sexual assault may well interpret these purity statements—laid out so carefully in the pages of their sacred scripture—as a powerful affirmation from on high of their *own* defilement and worthlessness in God's eyes. And that, I contend, is the *truly* shameful thing about this purity discourse.

Victim blame and "hardwired" men

As I mentioned near the start of this chapter, an important part of the evangelical purity discourse is that girls and women are positioned as having a naturally passive sexuality, while men are innately "hardwired" to pursue sex aggressively whenever they can. Evangelical teen girls are thus strongly discouraged from having a sexual self or even an interest in sexuality; sexual desire is not natural for girls, but rather is something that will lead to their ruin. In contrast, boys' desire for sex is inordinately natural, they have "an essential sexual appetite" that girls must learn to fend off (Fahs 2010, 120). Guys, it appears, are "visually stimulated" by the sight of female bodies (e.g. Gresh 2011; Ethridge and Arterburn 2004, 18–19), which are "created to contain sexual capital" (Stanley 2020, 120). A glimpse of female flesh (or even the suggestion of it) is enough to make a guy lose his godly inhibitions. Guys may also easily misinterpret girls' "overly" friendly behaviours and interactions; a smile, a wink, or a wave might be understood by guys as an invitation for some immediate sexual (and thus sinful) action.

Viewed through the lens of this purity discourse, girls' bodies are reduced to little more than a "stumbling block" for the unwitting males of the species—a source of "temptation" that drives boys and men to enact their God-given urge to have sex (Klein 2018, Introduction, Kindle).[13] Girls are cautioned to "protect" godly guys from sexual incontinence by embracing modest dress *and* behaviour: hiding their tempting bodies from the male gaze and self-policing their relationships, appearances, and actions. Spaghetti strap tops, plunging necklines, too-short shorts, low-rise jeans, and tight shirts, skirts, and trousers (tight *anything*, to be honest) are all strictly off-limits for evangelical teen girls. As are any behaviours deemed "flirty" or "attention-seeking." In essence, girls are rendered responsible for both their own sexual purity *and* the purity of their Christian brothers (Klein 2018, ch. 6, Kindle). As Stanley observes, "For centuries, then, modesty has been envisioned as obedience to God, in a gendered regime where unruly bodies are reined in, through disciplining girls' dress and deterring their desires. Christian girls are constructed as bodies that must be brought under control to guard good, Christian boys" (2020, 122).

In the strange and contradictory world of purity discourse, girls are therefore both totally powerless and utterly power*ful*—"victims of sexuality" who lack any real agency or subjectivity to negotiate their sexual boundaries (Fahs 2010, 120), but also "keepers" of a dangerously potent sexual allure which must remain hidden in order to protect godly men (Gresh 2011). "As young girls," notes Stanley, "we learn that we are rewarded by the male gaze. In a commodified body economy, glances are as good as gold" (2020, 120). Girls, however, are warned not to gather too much of this "gold," or proactively seek it out. For if a guy is tempted to sexually sin—if his male gaze falls upon a girl and gives him cause to "stumble"—then it's more than likely he has been driven to do so by the girl's appearance or behaviour. His desires are God-given, don't forget, so he really cannot be held accountable for doing what God "hardwired" him to do when the opportunity presents itself. As such, girls' and women's embodied presence is constructed as a source of spiritual danger for godly men, and must remain both controlled *and* hidden to protect Christian brothers from temptation.

This message echoes throughout the teen girl Bibles I looked at, as well as in the various books, websites, and video channels devoted to teen girl purity and modesty.[14] Girls have to keep their bodies suitably covered lest they (wittingly or unwittingly) attract the male gaze; they must also avoid "flirting" or appearing too "keen," as guys will read this as an invitation for some form of sexual encounter. In one *True Images* "In Focus" profile, titled "Sending a Message," Isabel reports that her cousin Johanna dresses in tight-fitting and revealing clothing and "gets all sorts of attention" (*TIB* 605). Hungry for some male attention of her own, Isabel heeds Johanna's advice, that "you've got to send a message to guys to let them know you're available." And true enough, as soon as she wears an outfit that "shows off" her figure, guys start flirting with her "big time." The editorial response to Isabel certainly affirms her beliefs—"When you dress sexy, you send a message"—but warns readers that this will only lead to trouble: "If you don't want to be seen as a sex object, then don't advertise your body by trying to get guys to want you sexually." The response assumes girls choose to dress in certain ways *only* to attract boys, rather than to fit in with their female peer group or simply to enjoy looking good. Girls' bodies, it seems, are only for the male gaze, and as such, are a source of girls' shame.

Isabel's profile also assumes that girls hold the power to control whether or not they receive the male gaze; the use of the terms "sex object" and "advertise" identify girls' bodies as a commodity that they use to "tempt" and attract male attention. The possibility that girls want to dress however they wish *without* receiving such attention is not even considered, nor is the idea that girls have the right to tell creepy, ogling guys to go away. And while readers are assured that "there's no harm in looking good," they are also reminded that "Christians are supposed to focus on what's noble, right and pure"—things that teen girl bodies clearly are not, unless they are adequately hidden from view and attract the least amount of attention. The profile ends with the advice, "Think twice about what you're wearing and develop the habit of seeking God's approval, not the stares of guys around you" (*TIB* 605). Again, the assumption made here is that teen girls have the agency and power to control the male gaze. So, if they receive it, even when they do not want it, it's still their fault.

The idea that girls actively *seek out* the male gaze is reinforced elsewhere in *True Images*. In another "In Focus" profile (titled "Shameless"), Mackenzie admits that, now she has a bit of cleavage, she is "not ashamed to show it off" (*TIB* 1206). While friends give her grief for "being a flirt," Mackenzie doesn't care: "I'll give the guys *almost* anything they want as long as I get what I want in return—popularity, attention, a date to every dance. It's all a game, and for once, I'm winning" (emphasis original). The editorial advice warns readers not to follow Mackenzie's lead of being "obsessed with getting attention," assuming once more that girls' main concern about their bodies is to attract the male gaze. For even if girls want to seek out male attention, they are told that this is ungodly and sinful behaviour. Girls are again made to feel shame about their bodies and their sexual agency.

Girls' engagement with the male gaze is also brought up in a *Bible for Teen Girls* devotional on the adulterous temptress in Proverbs 7:10 (*BTG* 788).[15] Taken from a book (*Pure Love, Pure Life*) by Elsa Kok Colopy (2012), the author recalls walking along the boardwalk one day when she was a teenager, "wearing a sports bra with a light knit top over it. My top kept sliding off one shoulder and I remember the boys walking by, glancing over and letting their eyes drop. Their attention brought a sense of confidence and excitement—an adrenaline rush." Colopy's initial elation, however, evaporated when she realized that "we were all using each other that day. I was using the guys to feel good about myself. The guys were using me for a quick thrill." She then gives readers the following advice: "If this is an issue for you, you have to take some time to figure out why it's so important to *tempt your guy or draw the gaze of guys* who walk past" (emphasis added). If a girl wears something comfortable, something she enjoys wearing, something appropriate for a warm summer's day, she is *still* being a temptress if men choose to look at her. She is the one "drawing the gaze," and it is assumed that she will welcome it. But if that gaze is unwanted, it is still her fault. There is no attempt here to problematize the gaze of random men looking at a teenage girl's bra strap—they are let entirely off the hook because *she* is the one inciting their gaze, so *she* must own the shame. Readers are told at the end of this devotional to "Ask God to show you why you might be making the decision to draw attention to your body," again reinforcing the idea that girls control and invite the male gaze.

This theme is taken up again in another *Bible for Teen Girls* devotional focusing on modest dress ("Dressed to Thrill ... God," *BTG* 828). Taken from a book by Crystal Kirgiss (*More than Skin Deep*, published in 2011), the author repeats Colopy's theory that teen girls dress in a certain way because they enjoy male attention. Kirgiss cautions girls that their clothes should not be "intentionally sexy," "intended to entice a guy's eyes," "intended to 'flaunt it if you've got it'" or "something that says, 'Please, please, look at me—you're going to like what you see'." For Kirgiss, then, girls "flaunt" their bodies to "entice" men, actively inviting male attention. Again, she echoes Colopy (and the *True Images* profiles), crediting teen girls with the superpower to control the male gaze, while simultaneously shaming them for it.

Absent from these modesty discussions is any mention of consent (Fahs 2010, 121); instead, teenage sexuality is presented as a hunting ground, where girls must wrap their sexuality in camo gear, while guys stalk around, searching for prey. This "erotic warfare" narrative peppers girls with "alarmist discourses" about "dangerous" and "dirty" sex, all the while assuring them that someday, they will want to marry one of those guys from whom they are currently hiding (Pillow 2004, 176; cited in Fahs 2010, 121). Such rhetoric is heavily dependent on traditional heteronormative gender stereotypes that subordinate women to male power and control; it reinforces the idea that "men should control women's bodies and their sexuality" (Klement and Sagarin 2017, 219), and denies girls any sense of their own sexuality or their right to authentic sexual expression (Valenti 2009, 175–76). Framing teen girls' sexuality as something potentially treacherous for men also offers the ideal excuse to police and control girls' behaviour, to shame them into foregoing their sexual autonomy and agency, and to reinforce these same gendered stereotypes that demand women's subjugation.

So, while modesty teachings try to tell girls that *they* hold a dangerous power over men's sexual and spiritual wellbeing, these teachings ultimately aim to subvert that power, insisting to girls that their own sexuality is far too "dangerous" to remain uncontrolled and unfettered. The reality is, of course, that teenage girls typically have little or no power, sexual or otherwise—the idea that they do is just part of the wider purity myth. But by teaching girls that their sexual agency *does* have powerful capital, and that it *always* poses a potential threat to godly Christian men, purity and modesty proponents can draw on religious authority to justify why girls' sexuality must be proscribed and controlled.

More than this, though, modesty discourse and the stereotypes underpinning it also help to affirm rape myths that blame victims for their own sexual assaults and exonerate the perpetrators (Klement and Sagarin 2017, 215). As we saw in the examples earlier, modesty messaging teaches teen girls that if they receive male sexual attention, it is essentially their fault: the male gaze is never unsolicited, whether girls realize this or not. And, by logical extension, this is just as true when male attention is unwanted or unwelcome (Klement and Sagarin 2017, 219). Teen girls must therefore be accountable for their *own* bodily and sexual integrity, not to mention protecting men from their God-given "urges" to rape women.

Rather like the rhetoric that frames rape victims as "damaged goods," the propensity to hold rape victims accountable for their assault is all too common in wider culture and has been for a long time. The belief that victims (of all genders, but particularly female) must have been "asking for it" is one of the most pervasive and widely held rape myths in many cultures and communities. Implicit in this myth is the assumption that, through her behaviour or appearance, the victim must have "encouraged" or "provoked" her rapist, or given the rapist the "wrong impression" that she was indeed willing to have sex

(Edwards et al. 2011, 766–67). What the victim was wearing, doing, saying, where she was walking, how much she'd had to drink, if she was taking drugs, if she had any sort of past sexual history—all of this is considered relevant in deciding how "innocent" she is, and how much "guilt" the rapist should shoulder, or even if what happened should actually count as a "real rape." In other words, defining a sexual act as a sexually *violent* act often depends in large part on the behaviour, appearance, and *personhood* of the victim herself.

Now, to be sure, the editorial additions in some of the teen Bibles I looked at do make explicit statements about rape and sexual abuse *never* being a girl's fault. An "In Focus" profile in *True Images*, for example, raises the issue of rape and tells readers, "Rape is never the victim's fault. Feelings of guilt are normal, but remember that the rapist is the only one guilty of a crime. *Nothing* someone wore, *nothing* someone said, *nothing* someone did could ever justify this crime" (*TIB* 148; emphasis original). These are commendable words to include, but they feel a little disingenuous, given *True Images*' emphatic teachings on modesty and the male gaze, which insist that men "can't help themselves" when girls show off their bodies and flirt. As Stanley notes ruefully, evangelical modesty rhetoric essentially drives home the message that "women's clothing can talk, it can actually ask for it" (2020, 120).

Moreover, the fictional girl in this profile, Ebony,[16] begins her story by saying, "There's no way I'm going to talk to my youth group leader or pastor about it, because I know I shouldn't have been at that party. I know I shouldn't have been drinking" (*TIB* 148). This surely serves to plant a seed of doubt in the reader's mind about the moral worthiness of this victim, laying at least some of the blame on her shoulders by virtue of her immodest behaviour. And while Ebony insists that she withheld her consent ("I do remember begging him to get off me and pleading with him not to take off my clothes. But I was powerless to stop him"), a later "Dare to Believe" note in this same Bible might cast further doubt on her innocence, as it warns teen girls that drinking alcohol "makes you vulnerable to abuse, embarrassment and temptation. Don't *let yourself* be led into trouble" (*TIB* 837; emphasis added). Although sexual violence is not mentioned explicitly in this note, the suggestion is clear that girls who drink may play a role in their own victimization if they "let" bad things happen to them.[17]

Thus, despite their insistence to the contrary, teen girl Bibles like *True Images* reinforce the idea that female victims of sexual violence may need to shoulder at least some of the culpability for their own assaults, given these Bibles' repeated insistence that women tempt men to sexual sin through their actions or appearance, and that men may respond aggressively because they "just can't help themselves." Girls' and women's bodies thus become inscribed as sites of sin, even when these same bodies are traumatized by sexual assault. If a rape victim was dressed "immodestly," or was too friendly or flirty, or was drinking alcohol at a party, then she has to take at least some of the blame. As Klein argues, "When we demand that an individual dress in just the right way so as not to inspire sexual feelings in others, we set a precedent of blaming individuals for the thoughts, feelings, and actions of other people that can play out in dangerous ways in rape and abuse cases" (2018, ch. 4, Kindle).

This discourse of victim blame has a devastating impact on the young women at the receiving end of it, but it also has an insidious effect on the boys and men who hear it. As Klein notes, although purity culture messaging is often different for boys and girls, both will be aware of what the other is hearing: "Boys hear girls being told that they must cover their bodies and avoid flirtation in order to protect themselves from boys' and men's uncontrollable sexual virility" (2018, ch. 13, Kindle). This sends a powerful message to young men that their abusive behaviour towards girls and women is justified, or even expected of them. Or, as Valenti puts it more bluntly, it suggests to men that they are "little more than walking dicks" (2009, 175). It also encourages boys to make the logical leap that any girl or woman who does get sexually assaulted was likely "asking for it" due to her appearance or behaviour, and is therefore at least partly (if not fully) to blame (Klein 2018, ch. 13, Kindle).

And certainly, in evangelical teen guy Bibles, this rhetoric of boys being "hardwired for sex" and unable to "help themselves" comes across very strongly. I took a peek at the *Revolution* Bible for teen guys (Zondervan's male counterpart to *True Images*) and there are numerous examples of this messaging being offered to teen guys. The introductory notes to Song of Songs, for example, reassure readers that "God is available 24/7 to help you when your appetite for sex gets *out of control*" (*Revolution* 857; emphasis added). Another note on the opposite page (titled "Learning Self-Control," 856) reminds guys to take it easy: "God has wired you to want to have sex; and once you start 'rounding the bases' and physically heading in that direction, it's hard to put on the brakes … Learn to appreciate your God-given sexual urges, but at the same time learn to practice self-control to get the best out of sex—after your wedding." In yet another editorial note about lust, guys are tasked with considering how to keep their thoughts pure when they are "faced with temptation" (*Revolution* 1479). "It seems like everywhere you look, there's something to tempt you to think impure thoughts," guys are told, "so how do you engage the world and interact with women without lusting?" Although this editorial also stresses that "women don't exist to serve your physical desires," the constant messaging about young men having an insatiable (and perfectly acceptable) sexual appetite that is vulnerable to female temptation only confirms the rhetoric of victim blame implicit in wider purity and modesty discourses.

This rhetoric of victim blame and perpetrator exoneration found in evangelical teen girl (and guy)Bibles sends a powerful message to their readers: rape is just another word for sinful sex—an inevitable response of men towards women who do not follow the tenets of purity culture (Klement and Sagarin 2017, 220). Purity discourse teaches teen girls that they are liable to be blamed for their rape/abuse if they make their own choices about what to wear, where to go, how to act with others: in other words, if they show a grain of agency, they are blamed for the "consequences," regardless of how serious these may be. The power, control, and violence that underlie every act of sexual violence are therefore erased, the perpetrator is excused, and the victim is blamed and shamed. As I discuss in the following chapter, by interweaving purity culture and rape culture discourses together, these teen girl Bibles (and the various books produced by the purity industry) are effectively erasing sexual violence.

Conclusion

The evangelical purity movement is dreadfully worried about teenage girls having sex. Indeed, teen girl sexuality is something of an obsession. While purity proponents level a great deal of criticism against the hypersexualization and commodification of girls in our "sex-saturated" culture, the purity movement itself seems just as invested in this same process. As Valenti notes, "There's an awful lot of talk about girls' sexuality in the movement … By focusing on the virginity of young women and girls, the movement is doing exactly what it purports to abhor—objectifying women and reducing them to their sexuality" (2009, 62; also Fahs 2010, 167; Stanley 2020, 120; Moslener 2017, 610). The virginity movement, argues Valenti, "is fighting sexualization [of girls] with more sexualization—we just don't always recognize it as such because it's shrouded in language about modesty, purity, and protection" (2009, 62). Or as Heather Hendershot observes, "prochastity media makes ignoring sex impossible" (2004, 99).

As I have shown throughout this chapter, the evangelical purity discourse articulated in teen girl Bibles is deeply problematic. It measures a girl's moral worth according to her sexual status; it proscribes and prescribes girls' behaviour, denying them sexual agency; it shames girls for wanting to claim any sexual and bodily autonomy; it blames girls when they are sexually assaulted, and exonerates the perpetrator; it makes victims of sexual violence feel damaged and shamed; and it perpetuates gender stereotypes that keep girls and women subordinated and under male control. As Breanne Fahs notes, the evangelical purity-driven conceptualization of female sexuality:

> results in a highly gendered social space that reinforces women's oppressed sociosexual status as the property of men, inadequately prepares them for negotiating the terms of their sexual health, and encourages them to seek out chastity clubs and social spaces that construct an identity based on enforced repression of sexual desire and expression. As such, issues of personal agency—for example, the extent to which women *choose*, or, alternatively, are *pushed into* these social spaces—represent a crucial problem in the culture of chastity.
>
> (117; emphasis original)

Moreover, this fixation on teen girls' purity (as though it were the most important and urgent issue girls had to deal with) takes attention away from the myriad social issues and forms of violence many girls experience every day: sexual violence and abuse, family violence, poverty, lack of access to reproductive healthcare, bullying, harassment, and racism, to name but a few. What kind of world could the politically powerful evangelical Christian community make if it chose to tackle these issues instead? As Valenti notes:

> If the same people who are working themselves into a purity panic over women's sexuality spent half as much time advocating on behalf of issues that young women really need help with, we might actually be getting somewhere. But instead, we're stuck talking about what a shame it is that young women are having sex, when the truth is, it isn't a shame at all.
>
> (2009, 189–90)

Proponents of the evangelical purity movement may clutch their pearls at teen pregnancies and sexually transmitted infections, but if they really want to help teen Christians negotiate this "sex-saturated" culture with their mental, spiritual, and physical health intact, they need to stop pushing abstinence-only rhetoric and offer all young people proper access to comprehensive safer sex education. Teenagers need to be equipped to make informed decisions about their sexual health, including access to appropriate contraception, negotiating consent, and recognizing healthy (and unhealthy) sexual relationships. The constant messaging that premarital sexual activity is dirty and shameful only causes untold harm (Fahs 2010, 137). It shames, blames, and stigmatizes girls who choose a sexual life, as well as those who are victims of sexual harm. It teaches girls and young women that their bodies are nothing more than objects that men can use to act out their "God-given" sexual needs. It perpetuates harmful gender stereotypes that deify female subordination and sexual passivity while exonerating male sexual aggression. And it erases sexual assault from evangelical Christian discourse, framing it alongside any other "immoral" sexual act that stains the participants with sin and guilt.

Don't get me wrong: I have no issue with sexual abstinence per se. It's as valid a lifestyle choice as any other, and I would never shame anyone (teen girl or otherwise) who chooses to follow this path. But that's the thing, it has to be a *choice*. Teen girls' sexuality needs to be recognized as a potentially "positive part of [their] youthful identity," rather than "a problem to be managed" (Allen 2005, 390; see also Allen 2013, 295). Rather than shaming teen girls about having a sexuality and a body, evangelical Christian communities would be better served equipping these girls with the agency and resources to look after their sexual selves and to make safe, realistic, and informed choices.

Notes

1 For a detailed discussion of the history of the purity movement in the evangelical Christian tradition, see Moslener (2015), who traces its roots and development in the United States back to the nineteenth century.
2 Space does not allow me to discuss the many books and devotionals aimed at teen girls, which likewise promote this evangelical purity discourse. Some notable examples include works by Dannah Gresh (2011, 2012) and Shannon Ethridge and Stephen Arterburn (2004), which I refer to occasionally throughout this chapter. For scholarly discussion of these and other evangelical purity books for girls and young women, see Fahs (2010); Stanley (2020); Colgan (2018); Klement and Sagarin (2017).
3 In the heady world of purity balls, fathers pledge to safeguard the virginity of their prepubescent and teenage daughters until they are married. Girls typically make a reciprocal pledge, confirming that their father will "protect" their virginity until he hands it over to their future husbands. For more discussion of this particular purity culture commodity, see Valenti (2009, 65–69); Fahs (2010).
4 In an autoethnographic account of her own experiences growing up in a high school purity culture, Olivia Stanley (2020, 118) offers a wonderfully evocative description of the abstinence-only sex education she received at her conservative Christian school in New Zealand: "To learn the mechanics of our maturing bodies, we were sent to the science department and

given a graphic glimpse into the taboos of boys' wet dreams and girls' periods. This was accompanied by a video of a man and a woman sitting under a white sheet, bolt upright in bed, clasping hands like ghostly lovers. This, laughed our male science teacher, was sex."
5 Purity rings are perhaps one of the better-known purity culture commodities. As Moslener (2017) notes, US-based groups such as True Love Waits and Silver Ring Thing have made a popular ritual out of young people wearing purity rings to represent their commitment to a sex-free and spiritually pure life before marriage. The rings symbolize the wearers' "spiritual transformation and sexual status, as well as their hope for marital gratification" (Moslener 2017, 609).
6 As Klein notes, abstinence-only sex education in public schools (which has been federally funded to the tune of USD$2 billion since 1981, particularly during the Reagan, Clinton, and Bush administrations) has been shown to be ineffective in delaying young people's first sexual encounters or preventing teenage pregnancies and the contraction of sexually-transmitted diseases (2018, Introduction, Kindle; see also Valenti 2009, 101–20; Williams 2011, 418; Fahs 2010, 119, 123–24). This is confirmed by Santelli et al. (2017), whose review of US abstinence-only policies concludes that they are ineffective, violate adolescent rights, stigmatize or exclude many young people, and reinforce harmful gender stereotypes. Santelli et al. (2017) recommend that adolescent sexual and reproductive health education needs to be based on scientific evidence and understanding, public health principles, and human rights—none of which are prominent or prioritized in evangelical purity discourse. For more on the history of the abstinence-only sex education movement in recent US history and its impact on public school sex education, see Williams (2011).
7 A common myth peddled by the evangelical purity proponents (such as Gresh 2012) is the "sexual prosperity gospel" (Beatly 2019), which avers that couples who wait to have sex until they are married are rewarded by God with a fantastic spouse, the most incredible sex life, and perpetual wedded bliss. Klein counters this discourse with numerous narratives from women (including herself) whose own experiences of growing up in an evangelical purity culture have caused them serious sexual anxieties and problems in their relationships and marital lives (2018, Chs 7, 9, Kindle). As Klein observes, purity culture "has dedifferentiated shame and sex over years of messaging, observation, and experience" (2018, ch. 9, Kindle).
8 Ethridge and Arterburn dedicate a whole chapter of their book, *Every Young Woman's Battle*, to the dangers of masturbation for women (2004, 43–50).
9 Dannah Gresh warns her teen girl readers that "nothing ever good happens in the horizontal position" (2012, ch. 9, Kindle).
10 Gresh (2012) and Ethridge and Arterburn (2004) list a cornucopia of sexually sinful deeds, and drive home the relentless message that *total* avoidance of tempting behaviours and thoughts (e.g. spending time alone with guys, dressing immodestly, having a boyfriend, being friendly or "flirty" with guys, watching TV with sexual content) are the only ways to stay pure.
11 See also Gresh (2012, ch. 11. Kindle) and Etheridge and Arterburn (2004, 163–72) for examples of this equation between extramarital sex and disease.

12 Gresh describes sexual sin as "spiritual cancer" (2012, ch. 5, Kindle) and insists that "so-called, safe sex is one of the most dangerous activities that exist" (2012, ch.2, Kindle). Fahs (2010, 127–31) and Stanley (2020, 124) heavily critique the use of such misinformation as scare tactics to drive home deeply conservative sexual ideals.

13 As Klein (2018, Introduction, Kindle) notes, this idea of women being "stumbling blocks" for men is far from biblically based. The only text to refer to this concept in a sexual context is Matthew 5:27–29, where Jesus warns men not to look at a woman with lust in their hearts. Klein rightly argues that this biblical text says nothing about girls and women being the *cause* of a man's sexual "stumbling"; rather, it reinforces men's own responsibility to avoid such sin. Nevertheless, she suggests that biblical texts are misused so often to justify evangelical purity culture that, for many women raised in the evangelical tradition, the Bible has become "the literature of their trauma" (2018, Introduction, Kindle). See also Stanley (2020, 122) who likewise discusses the misuse of this biblical verse in evangelical purity rhetoric.

14 I don't have room in this slim volume to discuss the multiple online sources dedicated to promoting evangelical teen girl purity and modesty. But if readers are interested, some fascinating examples include "Lies Young Women Believe" (https://liesyoungwomenbelieve.com/) and the "Girls Defined Ministry" website (https://www.girldefined.com/blog) and YouTube channel (https://www.youtube.com/user/girldefined). Special thanks to Lily Van Buskirk who trawled through these and many more sites as research for this book.

15 "Then out came a woman to meet him, dressed like a prostitute and with crafty intent" (Proverbs 7:10, NIV).

16 It is intriguing that the name chosen for the rape victim here is one we would normally associate with a woman of colour. Rape is something so heavily conflated with impurity and shame, it's as though the editors of *True Images* couldn't bear to connect it with whiteness. "Ebony" evokes darkness and dark skin, which have long been equated throughout our colonial history with the idea(l) of "rapeable women" (see hooks 1998; cited in Valenti 2009, 45). I also noticed in the now out-of-print teen girl Bible, *Revolve: The Complete New Testament* (2003) that its profile about rape is accompanied by a photo of a tearful brown-skinned girl. The threat of impurity through sexual violence is apparently not colour blind.

17 This messaging is also particularly prominent in Etheridge and Arterburn (2004). While readers are told that rape is "never your fault," this is belied by the book's various stories of underage girls and young women being assaulted, threatened, touched, and groomed by men, only for them then to be blamed for this unwanted male attention because of their own "flirty" behaviour or immodest appearance. For further discussion and critique of the rape myths articulated in this book and others of a similar ilk, see Klement and Sagarin (2017).

2 Erasing rape in teen girl Bibles and contemporary culture

In this chapter, I explore the ways that evangelical teen girl Bibles may perpetuate the common myth that sexual violence is essentially "just sex"—sinful sex, to be sure, if it occurs outside of marriage, but sex nonetheless, rather than an act of violence and coercion. These Bibles often deny the reality of sexual violence, both by failing to acknowledge its presence in the biblical texts and by reframing it as a sexual purity problem rather than an assault on a woman's bodily integrity. That is, when sexual violence *is* acknowledged, it is primarily evaluated in terms of its repercussions on the sexual purity of the (female) victim; she may be blamed, and even if she's not, she is no longer deemed to be chaste or pure as the result of her (albeit non-consensual) participation in premarital sex (Klein 2019, ch. 4, Kindle). This loss of purity is presented to teen girl Bible readers as the most traumatic aspect of sexual assault.

Given the persistent messaging in these Bibles about the importance of sexual purity, this evaluation of sexual violence should come as no surprise. Every sexual act (both consensual and coercive) is viewed through a purity lens; sexual (mis)deeds are regularly evaluated according to their impact on a teen girl's purity and virginity, rather than on her sexual integrity. When sex is seen as the *real* sin, sexual violence becomes just another threat to a girl's sexual purity, and thus a potential source of her stigma and shame. Consequently, the lines between consent and coercion are rendered unimportant—having consensual premarital sex becomes just as problematic as being raped (Fahs 2010, 122).

This erasure of rape is also achieved through the perpetuation of certain gendered discourses, which I discussed in the previous chapter. With guys "hardwired" to be sexually assertive and girls designed to be sexually submissive, rape becomes reimagined as natural and normal (Smart 1989, 41). A girl's "no" is translated as "yes," especially when she is deemed to be dressed immodestly or behaving in a way that is considered too friendly or "flirty." This social script sets women and girls up to be blamed for their sexual assaults; it also objectifies and commodifies female bodies, to the extent that sexual violence becomes eroticized as an inevitable feature of the healthy male libido, rather than being recognized as a criminal act of aggression (Burns 2005, 1–3; Blyth 2010, 39–43). As Heather Hendershot observes, "It sometimes seems that rape per se does not exist for fundamentalists. Instead, boys 'lose control' or 'force themselves' on girls" due to their God-given urges (2002, 92; cited in Fahs 2010, 121). Girls' sexual agency is thus effectively elided, as their every word and action are reinterpreted and reimagined through the lens of evangelical purity.

For the remainder of this chapter, I trace this elision of female sexual agency in my three teen girl Bibles. First, I outline the ways that these Bibles erase sexual violence in their profiles of biblical women and other editorial additions, by either ignoring it completely, reframing it as a purity concern, or blaming the victims for their own assaults. I then consider these Bibles' engagement with sexual violence in more contemporary contexts. Together, these features of teen girl Bibles send a potent message to their readers: rape is either your fault, or it's not worth mentioning in the first place—unless your purity is at stake.

Best left unsaid: silencing biblical victims of sexual violence

The Bible is full of gender violence. Its pages brim with traditions that witness the pervasiveness of sexual aggression and abuse within biblical Israel. Its narratives affirm the commonality of wartime rape, forced marriage, and sex slavery; there are stories of stranger rape, acquaintance rape, and gang rape (both threatened and actualized). The prophetic literature draws on metaphorical renditions of spousal abuse and intimate partner violence, perpetrated (or at least sanctioned) by Israel's jealous deity. The law codes uphold the structural violence of patriarchal power, which grants divine mandate to the rigidly prescriptive and proscriptive control of women's (and sometimes vulnerable men's) bodies. In essence, these ancient traditions testify to the subjective violence of multiple gendered abuses and grant a voice to the symbolic violence of misogynistic and heteronormative discourses, which marginalize and objectify women (and sometimes men), while normalizing their social, sexual, and religious subjugation.[1]

In the three teen girl Bibles I looked at, this biblical abundance of gendered violence is not always acknowledged. Time and again, depictions of rape and sexual abuse are reframed as stories of (typically women's) sexual sin and infidelity; on other occasions, these depictions are simply passed over without comment, particularly when the perpetrator is a biblical "hero" (such as Abraham, Hosea, or even the deity himself). Such an erasure of sexual violence serves to keep it under wraps, denying its ubiquity in the biblical texts and discouraging discussions of its pervasive presence in contemporary culture. As in so many other contemporary cultural texts, a thick and impenetrable silence surrounds sexual violence in teen girl Bibles, perpetuated by the shame and stigma so often associated with this crime. The elision of rape in these Bibles also serves to sustain the harmful myths and misperceptions that scaffold rape cultures—myths and misperceptions that blur the lines between consensual and coercive sex, blame (or disbelieve) victims, and exonerate perpetrators. When no one is talking about sexual violence, or listening to its victims, it is so much easier to ignore, to pretend it's not even happening, or to simply dismiss it as something that is not really worth noticing.

In the sections below, I discuss some of the biblical texts that depict sexual violence, illustrating how my three teen girl Bibles often erase or reinterpret this violence in ways that keep it wrapped in an insidious and troubling silence.

Genesis 16 and 21

In Genesis 16, Sarah takes steps to secure progeny for her husband Abraham.[2] Earlier in the Genesis narrative, God promised Abraham that he would become a "great nation" (Genesis 12:2) and that his descendants would be as numerous as the "dust of the earth" (Genesis 13:16). Yet Sarah remains sceptical; conscious that she is beyond childbearing age, she instructs Abraham to have sex with her Egyptian slave Hagar so that he can impregnate *her* to produce an Abrahamic heir (Genesis 16:2). In due course, Hagar becomes pregnant (v.4) and the power dynamic between her and Sarah shifts, to the point that Sarah begins treating Hagar (more) harshly, and Hagar runs away (v.6). After encountering an angel of the Lord who commands her to return to Sarah and "submit" to her, Hagar does as she is told and eventually bears Abraham a son, whom he calls Ishmael (v.15). Later, in Genesis 21, Sarah gives birth to her own son, Isaac, and for reasons left unclear in the biblical text, she then tells Abraham to evict Hagar and Ishmael from the family home (Genesis 21:8–10). Abraham obliges (after first consulting God), and dismisses the slave mother and her son (vv.11–13). The pair wander around the wilderness until their water runs out, and Hagar fears they will both perish. But at the last moment, an angel of the Lord arrives to shows her the location of a well (vv.14–19). Hagar and Ishmael then disappear from the Genesis narrative, but readers are reassured that God has promised them a future of their own (vv.20–21).

In much traditional biblical scholarship, Hagar's treatment by Sarah and Abraham in Genesis 16 and 21 is passed over with little remark, or is framed in terms of its placement in the wider Abrahamic story, which culminates in the birth of Isaac and the subsequent origins of Israelite (and consequently, Christian) history. A number of feminist biblical scholars and theologians, however, have pointed out the oft-elided gender violence that is inherent within these narratives (e.g. Tamez 1986; Williams 1993; Weems 1998; Scholz 2010; Domoney-Lyttle 2019). As a foreign, Egyptian, female slave, Hagar is multiply oppressed in this story, the intersecting elements of her identity (her race, her gender, her slave status) rendering her utterly "other" and utterly powerless. Being Sarah's slave (and therefore Sarah's "property"), her body belonged to Sarah; she had no agency to grant her consent to be a surrogate mother for her master and mistress (Domoney-Lyttle 2019, 53–54). She could not refuse to have sex with Abraham, or to be impregnated by him, and had no say in determining her own, or her son's, eventual fate (she did not even have the agency to choose her son's name). We hear nothing of Hagar's opinions or emotions during these events, and as Zanne Domoney-Lyttle rightly observes, "Her existence as [Sarah's] slave limits her from resisting, objecting, or voicing her consent (or lack thereof). Even if she were to object or resist, her station as slave-girl likely means her resistance would not even have been acknowledged" (2019, 53).

Womanist biblical scholars and theologians, such as Renita Weems (1998), Elsa Támez (1986), and Delores Williams (1993), have noted the parallels that exist between Hagar's experiences and the social, economic, and sexual exploitation experienced by women of colour throughout history and up to the present day.[3] Given the white, middle-class roots of the evangelical community (mentioned in the Introduction), it should come as no surprise that Hagar's rape and exploitation are elided from the teen girl Bibles produced by this faith community. In *True Images*, for example, Genesis 16 is framed as a story highlighting Sarah's failure to have sufficient trust in God's plans, warning readers that if they try to "fix" their own problems (like Sarah did), they may end up in an "even bigger mess" (*TIB* 18). Sarah's "mess" is not defined in terms of her complicity in Hagar's rape; indeed, Sarah's "Mirror Images" profile focuses on her initial "doubts" in God but lauds her eventual turn to faith (*TIB* 22). And while there is some sympathy for Hagar expressed in *her* "Mirror Images" profile (*TIB* 77), her status as a victim of sexual assault is hidden beneath layers of obfuscation and victim blame. The profile acknowledges she is a "slave," but ignores her inability to consent to being impregnated by Abraham. Instead, readers are told that she "got stuck in the middle of a really bad situation," which implies a degree of complicity and suggests she is to blame (to some extent at least) for what happened to her. The profile does admit that Hagar was "mistreated" by Sarah (echoing Genesis 16:6), but describes this as nothing more than "an uncomfortable situation." Again, the violence experienced by Hagar is silenced and erased through obfuscation; rape and abuse become "situations" for which both Hagar and Sarah are culpable (Abraham seems to get off scot-free, as his rape of Hagar is never mentioned). Hagar, we are told, "didn't know how to take care of herself on her own, and she needed God's help." How Hagar was meant to "take care of herself" when she was a raped, pregnant, foreign, and ultimately abandoned female slave is left unexplained; instead, she is portrayed as a naive and unfortunate girl who made just as many bad choices as Sarah and Abraham. The profile ends with readers being reminded not to run away from their own problems, lest they become like Hagar, "sitting in the desert—going nowhere fast."

Hagar's rape is likewise erased in *Revolve*, which focuses solely on Sarah's desire to bear a child. In Sarah's "Ladies of the Bible" profile (*RB* 16), Sarah tells Abraham to "sleep with her slave girl" and when he agrees, she is delighted that she'll "finally have a baby!" While Hagar is identified as a "slave" here, her inability to consent to the couple's plan is, again, not mentioned; indeed, her voice is utterly elided from this conversation—she doesn't even get her own "Ladies of the Bible" profile. Interestingly, the heading for Genesis 16 used in the NCV translation ("Ishmael is born") similarly erases Hagar from her own narrative.

Meanwhile, the *Bible for Teen Girls* echoes *Revolve*'s focus on Sarah's desire for offspring; the devotional accompanying Genesis 15–16 tells readers that Sarah "concocted a plan" in order to acquire a "tiny baby," but her "troubles only got worse" (*BTG* 20). This devotional (an excerpt from the Zondervan book *Project Inspired* by Nicole Weider, 2015) does not even mention Hagar's role in Sarah's "plan," nor does it explain exactly what this plan entailed. Rather, Weider focuses on Sarah's impatience and her seeming lack of trust in God's promise. A couple of pages later, Hagar is given her own profile, where she is described as Sarah's "maid," rather than her slave (*BTG* 22). At least here, the Bible editors seem to acknowledge Hagar's exploitation: "Times were tough for Hagar. It didn't seem as if anyone truly cared about her. She was simply a pawn to be moved around on a giant chessboard in a game other people were playing." Yet the language once again erases the gendered violence inherent in this event; there is no mention of rape or sexual coercion, and like *True Images*, the real problem is seen as Sarah's failure to trust in God, rather than her complicity in the sexual abuse of her slave.[4]

This erasure of sex slavery likewise occurs in *True Images*' brief mention of Bilhah and Zilpah, the slaves of Jacob's wives Rachel and Leah. Like Hagar, Bilhah and Zilpah were "given" to Jacob by his wives so that he might impregnate them (Genesis 30). In Rachel's "Mirror Images" profile (*TIB* 199), readers learn that she was "competing" with Leah to see who could give Jacob the most male progeny: "Rachel forced her servant-girl [Bilhah] to have more babies in her stead just to keep pace with the fertile Leah." While the word "forced" is used here, the profile does not explicitly allude to rape, nor does it even mention Zilpah or *her* rape at the hands of Jacob after Leah's intervention. Instead, Rachel is simply chastised for her over-competitive behaviour. Similarly, *Revolve* mentions "poor Bilhah," and laments that "she was hardly even treated like a human being at all. She felt invisible, as if her true self didn't matter to anyone on earth" (*RB* 34). Yet *Revolve* editors seem decidedly coy when it comes to talking about sexual violence, leaving readers to work out for themselves why Bilhah deserves their sympathy

Genesis 34

While the rape of Dinah is afforded no editorial mention in *Revolve* or the *Bible for Teen Girls*, this narrative is one of the few instances in *True Images* where biblical sexual violence is explicitly recognized and discussed (similarly, Tamar in 2 Samuel 13, whom I discuss later). *True Images* uses the NIV translation, which adopts the term "rape" in Genesis 34:2 to describe Dinah's sexual assault by the Canaanite prince Shechem,[5] and each time Dinah is mentioned in an editorial note, her status as rape victim is acknowledged. In a "Dare to Believe" note (*TIB* 44), readers are reminded that "Rape is never the victim's fault." "But," it continues, "in some circumstances you can take steps to help keep yourself safe. Make wise decisions." Any outright rejection of victim blame is tempered here by the suggestion that girls are responsible (at least in part) for *not* getting raped; the logical conclusion we can draw from the "Make wise decisions" edict is that any girl who *is* raped may have not been "wise." The note does not expand on what "wise decisions" entail but going by the pervasive purity rhetoric found elsewhere in this Bible (as discussed in Chapter 1), I would infer that they involve a girl dressing modestly and desisting from "flirty" behaviour with the opposite sex. There is no mention of the rapist here, no assertion of his culpability or *his* need to make the "wise decision" to *not* rape women.

Dinah's "Mirror Images" profile does, I must admit, go some way to repairing the damage. Titled "Love's Not Like That" (*TIB* 130), it acknowledges that Shechem sexually assaulted Dinah: "Dinah knew the pain of abuse and the confusion that results from someone talking one way and acting another. It's agonizing and devious, and it's just not right." Dinah is exonerated of any culpability, and the myth of victim blame is dismissed for contemporary readers too: "If you've experienced any type of abuse—sexual, physical, emotional or verbal—know it's not your fault, just as what happened to Dinah wasn't her fault." It's a relief, at least, that this profile does not follow the common trend in biblical scholarship of holding Dinah accountable for her rape because she "went out" by herself to meet some local women (Genesis 34:1).[6]

Dinah's "Mirror Images" profile (*TIB* 130) also insists that "abusive relationships are about power. Some relationships turn violent and some are more about manipulation and control. In any of these unhealthy dynamics, it's wrong and destructive. It happens between married couples and in families, and it also happens in dating relationships." The profile recognizes different types of abusive relationships in contemporary contexts, reiterating that these are *always* damaging and wrong. This is a welcome and valuable message to impart to teen girl readers (not least of all the acknowledgment of spousal abuse). Nevertheless, as I discuss further in this chapter and again in Chapter 3, it is somewhat undermined by the editorial additions found elsewhere in this Bible, which repeatedly echo and normalize the same manipulative and abusive rhetoric employed by perpetrators of sexual harm and coercive control. After reading my way through *True Images*, this profile's disapproval of power-based abuse started to ring more than a little hollow.

Genesis 39

Genesis 39 recounts the attempted rape of Joseph while he is a slave in the Egyptian household of Potiphar, one of the Pharaoh's military officials. After repeatedly harassing him to have sex with her (vv.7–10), Potiphar's wife tries to grab Joseph and force herself upon him, but he manages to escape (vv.11–12), so she then accuses him of attempting to rape *her* (vv.13–18). This narrative is one of three Hebrew Bible stories that recount the threat of male rape; the other two texts (Genesis 19 and Judges 19) are not discussed at all in the three teen girl Bibles I surveyed, but Joseph's ordeal at the hands of Potiphar's wife is brought up in several editorial additions and notes. In most cases, the sexual coercion explicit in this text is elided, and the story is reframed as a cautionary tale about the dangers of premarital sex and predatory female sexuality.

For example, in a *True Images* "Dare to Believe" note referencing Genesis 39:9, readers are reminded that "Sex outside of marriage has all kinds of consequences—unplanned pregnancy, sexually transmitted infections and broken hearts—but worst of all, it hurts God" (*TIB* 52). Joseph's threatened rape becomes the threat of premarital sex, as though the two were somehow synonymous. This is reiterated in the *Bible for Teen Girls*, where Joseph is lauded for "flee[ing] an easy opportunity to sin" (*BTG* 55). Joseph, it appears, was not running away from a threatened sexual assault, he was fleeing sexual temptation. For the editors of these Bibles, the most significant thing about rape is clearly *not* the threat it poses to victims' sexual agency or bodily autonomy, but rather its potentially damaging impact on their sexual purity.

This reconfiguration of rape as a sexual purity issue is reiterated in a *True Images* "Genuine Note," where Potiphar's wife is described as attempting to "seduce" Joseph, who in turn "chose to stay sexually pure" (*TIB* 52). Again, sexual aggression is silenced, drowned out by purity rhetoric, and Joseph's efforts to fend off Potiphar's wife are explained in terms of his desire to retain his sexual purity, rather than to avoid being raped. Teen girl readers are reminded in this note that, every day, they "face choices like Joseph. Will you dress, talk and act in a way that honors God?" This discourse of "choice" is disturbing, as it ignores Joseph's status as a slave in Potiphar's house, suggesting that if he had "chosen" not to flee, his sexual encounter with his slave owner's wife would have been utterly consensual. It also peddles the same victim-blaming rhetoric we see elsewhere in *True Images*: girls are assumed to have "choice" and agency over who has access to their bodies and sexuality; their appearance and behaviour is framed as the reason that boys might try to "seduce" them. The natural conclusion, then, is that if girls face similar harassment to Joseph, it really is their fault. And if they, unlike Joseph, fail to escape their "seducer," then they have made the wrong "choice" and damaged their sexual purity.

Potiphar's wife is given her own "Ladies of the Bible" profile in *Revolve*, which retells the events of Genesis 39 from her point of view.

In this creative rendition, she "checked out" Joseph because "he's younger and better looking than the other slaves—he's got a totally built, tan body. He just stands out as Mr. Cool and Capable" (*RB* 47). With a disturbingly salacious tone, readers are informed that "each day her mind races with thoughts of getting alone with him. She approaches him from behind, moving her hands up his back ... She tells him to come to bed with her, coiling her hand around his arm." Joseph's response to her harassment ("It is a sin against God," he insists) reframes his anxieties as concern for his sexual purity; despite being a slave, he shows no alarm at being non-consensually touched by or coerced into having sex with this privileged and powerful woman. Potiphar's wife continues to sexually harass him ("Day after day, she follows him, brushing up against him as he works"), and when she eventually "grabs" his coat, this event is described as a "seduction" and a source of "temptation" for Joseph, rather than an attempted rape. Again, the power disparity between these two characters is both acknowledged and elided, and girls are left with the message that they too should "say no to temptation," as though sexual harassment and abuse will "tempt" girls to sexually sin.

This *Revolve* profile also reminds readers that Potiphar's wife "makes up her story ... that [Joseph] tried to rape her" because she is worried what Joseph will tell her husband; she also wants to get back at the "common slave" who made her "feel undesirable and foolish" (*RB* 47). This is one of the few times that *Revolve* uses the word "rape" in *any* of its editorial discussions. Mentioned only when it did *not* happen, rape is thus reframed as simply something women will lie about—something that doesn't really exist. This profile therefore reinforces another common myth prevalent in contemporary rape cultures: that women often make false accusations of rape against wholly innocent men (Edwards et al. 2011, 767–68; Gilmore 2019, 88–89).

True Images also gives Potiphar's wife her own profile, where she is described as a manipulative woman who "pursued" Joseph "to have sex with her" (*TIB* 222). The choice of grammar here is interesting; she does not "pursue" him in order to have sex with *him*, but so that *he* can have sex with *her*. The evangelical insistence that women must be sexually passive is not quite shaken off here, despite the dubious morality of Potiphar's wife. And the use of the verb "pursue" to describe her harassment carries romantic rather than coercive overtones. The only hint of her sexual aggression comes in the next sentence, which tells us that when Joseph failed to comply with her demands, "she tried to *force* him to be with her" (emphasis added). When this does not work, she takes her "revenge," playing the "innocent victim," and using Joseph's cloak to "frame him as a rapist." Again, the only time that rape gets mentioned in this story is when it did *not* happen—it is something made up by a manipulative woman who apparently has "issues" and wants to get back at the man who "humiliated" her. Indeed, this profile invites *True Images* readers to see themselves as similar to Potiphar's wife, because her "strategies are alive and well today." The readers' prayer that accompanies the profile directs teen girls to pray: "Dear God, I often want to spin the truth, not tell it. Forgive me and teach me the value of always telling the truth." Girls, it seems, like to lie about rape—and a whole lot of other things too.

Judges 19–21

Judges 19–21 records a series of horrific sexual crimes, beginning with the fatal gang rape of an unnamed woman who is married to a Levite.[7] The Levite and his wife are travelling home to Ephraim and stop for the night in the Benjaminite town of Gibeah, where they meet a man who offers to host them for the night (19:16–21). A short time later, the men of the town surround the house and demand that the Levite come out so that they can rape him (v.22). The host remonstrates with the mob, offering them his virgin daughter and the Levite's wife in place of the Levite (vv.23–24). When the men of Gibeah refuse to accept this, the Levite grabs his wife and throws her out the door; she is then gang raped throughout the night (v.25). In the morning, she finds her way back to the house before collapsing on the doorstep; when her husband finds her, he tells her to "Get up," but she does not respond (v.27). He then takes her home and dismembers her body into twelve pieces, which he sends out to each Israelite tribe as a call to civil war (v.29). This biblical text of terror does not clarify if she was dead before being dismembered, rendering an already brutal story all the more horrific. The woman's eventual death provokes nationwide outrage and the outbreak of a civil war against the tribe of Benjamin (Judges 20), which in turn leads to the mass abduction and wartime rape of hundreds of young women from the Israelite towns of Jabesh Gilead and Shiloh (Judges 21).

Of the three teen girl Bibles I looked at, only one includes any editorial notes on Judges 19–21. *Revolve* includes a "Daily Devos" note ("Thank God for Security," *RB* 300), which reassures teen readers that "women's rights have come a long way since the Old Testament." The unnamed woman is described as the Levite's "slave," rather than his wife, and the NCV translation likewise describes her as a "slave woman." The precise meaning of the Hebrew word used to describe this woman's social status (*pîlegeš*) is widely disputed in biblical scholarship, although it is often translated as either "concubine" or "secondary wife" (see Paynter 2020, 14–15). Compared to the silence surrounding Hagar's rape, *Revolve* at least acknowledges this "slave" woman's sexual assault as "rape" and describes her husband's behaviour as "disgustingly unchivalrous"—an understatement for his complicity in her gang rape and dismemberment, but better than nothing, I suppose. The abduction of the young women at Shiloh is also acknowledged as "kidnapping," yet this editorial note refrains from engaging in any meaningful discussion about the sexualized violence inherent in these traditions, simply describing it as a "painfully sad story." Teen girl readers are advised to "Be thankful that you live in a time and place where you hopefully will never have to face a situation like this," and "don't take your freedom for granted." Girls are urged to use their God-given talents and abilities "for God's glory. Who knows, maybe you'll even end up defending the rights of abused and mistreated women in your nation or around the world." This is a nice enough sentiment, but the "be thankful" discourse is jarring, as though girls should be *grateful* for simply having "freedom" and for *not* being victims of gang rape, murder, or abduction. It also ignores the many teenage girls who *are* living in communities where they face daily threats or enactments of physical and sexual violence, or it assumes that girls who do are unlikely to read *Revolve*. This editorial note unwittingly exposes the multi-layered privileges (related to class, race, sexuality, and gender) that scaffold evangelical Christianity and help create the "ideal," middle-class, sexually pure Christian teen girl.

2 Samuel

The book of 2 Samuel includes two rape narratives that are discussed in various editorial sections of the three teen girl Bibles I looked at. The first of these, 2 Samuel 11, recounts David espying Bathsheba as she bathes on the roof of her house (vv.1–3). Despite the fact that she is married to Uriah, a soldier in the royal army, David sends for Bathsheba, has sex with her, and impregnates her (vv.4–5). When she tells him she is pregnant, he panics that his adultery will be discovered; after several fruitless attempts to persuade Uriah to sleep with his wife, David eventually orchestrates the soldier's death during battle (vv.6–17).

Was Bathsheba raped by David? Certainly, their encounter in 2 Samuel 11 is not depicted as explicitly violent or coercive: she "came to him" and he "lay with her" (v.4). Nevertheless, while the king may not have used physical force or the threat of violence to have sex with Bathsheba, the power imbalance that lay between these two characters would have compromised Bathsheba's ability to withhold her consent without fear of the consequences. This, in my view, renders it a case of coercive sexual intercourse that can be classified as a "rape."[8] But do the teen girl Bibles agree?

In its introductory notes to 2 Samuel, *True Images* admits that David "messed up big time. David slept with another man's wife" (*TIB* 363). In essence, then, David's adultery/rape of Bathsheba and his complicity in the murder of her husband Uriah is initially minimized to a "mess-up," which David regrets and for which he ultimately receives God's full forgiveness. Nevertheless, in Bathsheba's "Mirror Images" profile (*TIB* 718), the possibility of coercion is at least raised. "Bathsheba may have been starstruck and jumped at the opportunity to meet the most powerful man in her land," but on the other hand, "she may have been frightened. *Can I dare refuse the king?*" (emphasis original). Alone in the house, her husband off to battle, "How could she refuse to go" to the royal palace when David demanded her presence? In the next paragraph, however, we are told that the couple "slept together," which erases any hint of coercion and implicates Bathsheba in this adulterous act.[9]

While *True Images* recognizes the power imbalance between David and Bathsheba, it nonetheless refuses to name David's actions as tantamount to sexual assault. Bathsheba's "Mirror Images" profile ducks and dives between different positions, likening this story to girls who "make bad decisions" about "how far to go" with a guy they're infatuated with, but also mentioning the "terrible" things that can happen to a girl when they are "out for a walk, minding [their] own business"—an obtuse reference to stranger rape, I presume (*TIB* 718). Everything feels very confused and confusing—the reality of sexual violence is once again hidden by obfuscation and victim blame.

Meanwhile, in the *Bible for Teen Girls*, we encounter the same obfuscation regarding Bathsheba's possible rape. According to her "Women of the Bible" profile:

> Bathsheba may have been a faithful and godly woman. And maybe she wasn't. We don't know the exact details—in fact, we don't know anything about her response or feelings about the situation. But her life became very complicated very quickly. Most likely all of it happened against her will—it's not likely she could have refused the king or prevented pregnancy.
>
> (*BTG* 376)

At least here, the coercive nature of the encounter is identified as a *possibility*. But readers are left with a nagging doubt that "maybe" she wasn't so innocent after all, reinforcing the idea that women's experiences of sexual harm are *always* open to debate and doubt. And coercive or not, Bathsheba's story hearkens back to the same myths we have seen before in these teen Bibles—about men being unable to "help themselves" when they gaze upon a desirable woman. Because according to the *Bible for Teen Girls*, 2 Samuel 11 serves as "a reminder that it's easy for boys and men *to be tempted when they see something alluring*" (*BTG* 376; emphasis added). The implication is, then, that girls must prevent themselves from being "alluring" *and* from being seen.

Yet these preventative measures are still not enough to stop girls getting raped; Bathsheba's *Bible for Teen Girls* profile continues by saying that "even when we honor God with our bodies and our lives, others may violate and hurt us" (*BTG* 376). On those occasions, "God does not look away from you. He sees you, and he will heal you. No matter what has happened in your past, you can make choices that reflect godly inner beauty and modesty, being conscious of the God you represent. And trust that God will restore your life for his glory." Here, sexual violence is acknowledged, yet continues to be framed within the discourse of purity. Rape impacts, first and foremost, a victim's sexual purity, or chastity, rather than her physical and emotional wellbeing. And girls are reminded that they still have "choices" to stay modest, perhaps implying that they made "bad" choices in the past, which led to their sexual assault. Compounding this problematic discussion, the wording at the end—about God restoring a girl's life to "his glory"—only serves to reiterate the common myth that a girl's moral and spiritual identity is somehow damaged by her rape and needs to be "restored."

The *Revolve* Bible does a little better with Bathsheba, refusing to blame her for David's behaviour. Her "Ladies of the Bible" profile makes clear that she does not know David can see her bathing. Moreover, it notes that when he calls her to the palace, she may have been unable to refuse: "After all, he is the king, and in Bathsheba's world, women are rarely—if ever—asked for permission. If the king wanted her, he would have her" (*RB* 360). And while this profile admits that we cannot know what Bathsheba was thinking that night, "the whole situation likely made her feel like her life had—without her consent—suddenly become a chaotic mess." It is reassuring to see Bathsheba's lack of consent being raised explicitly here, but *Revolve* editors miss the opportunity to talk to teen girl readers about how they might deal with sexual coercion themselves. Instead, the advice given at the end of this profile is uselessly vague and impractical: "Sometimes things happen that are beyond your control, and you feel helpless and scared. Remember Jesus has been there, and he will never leave you!" This closing remark avoids mention of the sexual coercion implicit within this narrative; moreover, reassuring girls that "Jesus has been there" suggests (unintentionally perhaps) that they should simply put up with situations where they feel "helpless and scared," taking solace from the fact that Jesus has felt this way too.

The second rape narrative in 2 Samuel occurs in chapter 13, which recounts the rape of David's daughter Tamar by her half-brother Amnon. Amnon made himself sick lusting after Tamar, but because she was a virgin princess, she remained out of his reach (vv.1–2). Amnon's friend Jonadab therefore helps him to concoct a plan to be alone with Tamar (vv.3–5). Feigning illness, Amnon asks David's permission for Tamar to visit him with some health-giving cakes (v.6). David concurs and sends Tamar to Amnon's chambers, but once Tamar is in her half-brother's presence, he dismisses his servants then proceeds to rape her (vv.8–14). Afterwards, his love turns to hatred, and despite her heartbroken protestations, he has his servants throw her out of the house and bolt the door behind her (vv.15–18).

True Images includes several editorial notes about Tamar's rape. One "Dare to Believe" note (situated on the same page as the 2 Samuel 13 text) explicitly mentions Tamar's sexual assault: "Think the Bible's full of fairy tale stories and perfect endings? It's actually full of true stories and real-life experiences, like Tamar's rape. She felt the same shame and pain that many girls face today" (*TIB* 380). This note's mention of "shame" echoes the biblical narrative, which frames Tamar's rape as first and foremost a violation of her sexual chastity. In 2 Samuel 13:12–13, Tamar's initial response to Amnon's demand to "lie with" him focuses on the disgrace that will befall them both should they have sex outside of marriage; after the rape, she reiterates this when Amnon tells her to leave: "'No!' she said to him, 'sending me away would be a greater wrong than what you have already done to me'" (v.16). Thrown out of Amnon's house, she tears her robe (which we are told is the garment worn by virgin princesses), throws ash on her head, and wails, as though mourning her stolen virginity (vv.18–19). In the honour-shame culture of biblical Israel, Tamar is well aware that being an unmarried woman who is no longer a virgin is a huge source of personal shame and devaluation; this, rather than the violent rape itself, is what appears to upset her most. Indeed, after her assault, we are told that she stayed with her brother Absalom, living her life as "a desolate woman" (v.21).

The story of Tamar's rape drives home the devastating impact that purity culture has on victims of sexual assault. Despite the explicit violence of this event, the biblical narrator presents Amnon's assault as something that compromises his sister's purity, rather than as an attack on her bodily integrity and sexual autonomy. Situated within the purity-prioritising culture of biblical Israel, Tamar herself articulates the message that *she* must carry the shameful burden of no longer being a virgin. In her own eyes, as well as those of her rapist, she is devalued, despicable, unlovable—"damaged goods" whose future is reduced to a life of desolation and despair (vv.12–13, 16, 20). As a teaching text for teen girls, 2 Samuel 13 could serve as a powerful reminder of the emotional, psychological, and spiritual damage that purity rhetoric can inflict on women. In *True Images*, however, it is used to *affirm* this rhetoric rather than resist it.

True Images has a second "Dare to Believe" note placed on the same page as the one mentioned above, which does not mention her assault explicitly but curves back towards sex, alluding to the "love" that Amnon felt for Tamar, which led to his sexual assault. "Sometimes people will use the word 'love' in order to manipulate others," readers are told. "If a guy says he loves you just to get what he wants, then that is definitely not love" (*TIB* 380). True enough, but the coercion implicit in this situation is clouded with obscure references to "manipulation" and guys getting what they "want" (which, we presume, is sex). But rape isn't about guys getting what they "want," unless what they "want" is to hurt and control women. Rape is a crime fuelled by violence, not by sexual desire. But *True Images* ignores this, using Tamar's rape to warn girls not to compromise their sexual purity with any guy who whispers the L-word in their ear.

True Images also includes a "Mirror Images" profile for Tamar, which reiterates her status as a victim of rape (*TIB* 1089). It reminds readers that Amnon's claims to "love" his sister simply were not true: "Amnon's rape of Tamar had nothing to do with love. True love never hurts others or forces others to do things against their will. Rape is a violent crime against an innocent victim, and Tamar did nothing to provoke it. Not only did the rape hurt Tamar physically, but it also crushed her spirit and broke her heart." The profile rightly stresses the physical *and* psychic violence of rape; yet there is a terrible irony in the fact that Tamar's crushed spirit and broken heart have been caused to a large extent by the same purity culture rhetoric belaboured within the pages of this teen girl Bible.

Tamar's *True Images* profile goes on to note that girls today who experience sexual victimization may "carry the same emotional scars" as Tamar, feeling as though they are now "damaged goods" (*TIB* 1089). Readers are reassured that Christ can free them "from the disgrace of others' sins" perpetrated against them. The shame of rape is affirmed here, rather than being problematized; this shame belongs to the rapist, by rights, but victims are forced to carry it, as though it were their own. Through Christ, however, rape victims are reassured that they "can find freedom from shame and hopelessness. Freedom from feelings of bitterness and false guilt." Again, there is no recognition that at least some of this shame, hopelessness, and guilt may be *caused* in the first place by Christian evangelical purity teachings, which frame premarital sex (including non-consensual sex) as inherently shameful and implicate girls and women in their own victimization by virtue of their appearance and behaviour.

At the end of Tamar's "Mirror Images" profile, we are told that she "was never able to let go of her sadness and shame, and it shaped the rest of her life" (*TIB* 1089). The "customs of the time" did not allow her to marry after she had been raped, but fortunately, "girls today don't have to live with that same stigma." Don't they? *True Images* and other teen girl Bibles repeatedly reiterate "customs" and discourses that stigmatize and shame teen girls who fail to conform to strict purity teachings. The "customs" around virginity and sexual purity that sentenced Tamar to a life of desolation are alive and well in contemporary culture, including within evangelical communities. Even if they don't intend to, teen girl Bibles such as *True Images* help to ensure that contemporary victims of sexual violence will share Tamar's suffering with her.

Tamar's rape is not discussed in the *Bible for Teen Girls*, but it does get a brief mention in *Revolve*. Tamar's "Ladies of the Bible" profile (*RB* 364) describes this event in grimly voyeuristic detail; while the word "rape" is not used, there is mention of "force" and "violence" on Amnon's part. Tamar, we are told, feels "broken and used" after Amnon dismisses her, and she is left feeling burdened with "unbearable" grief and shame. Similar to *True Images*, Amnon's attack is put down to his "lust" and sexual "urges," while Tamar is described as "beautiful" and "young," as though this explains or excuses her brother's desire. Although the advice at the end of this profile tells girls that "violence against you is not your fault," we might be left with the impression that it is not Amnon's fault either, given Tamar's natural ability to inspire his lust.

The book of Esther

The book of Esther is not always identified as a text depicting sexual violence. Yet the second chapter of Esther relates the story of countless young women and girls (including Esther) who were gathered from across the empire and brought to the harem of the Persian king Ahasuerus. This was to allow him to choose a replacement for the deposed Queen Vashti, who was summarily dismissed after refusing to comply with the king's drunken demands (Esther 1:10–20). According to Ericka Dunbar (2019), Esther 2 depicts nothing short of sex trafficking and sexual exploitation instituted by the Persian empire on a global scale:

> Esther and countless other virgin girls are abducted from their native lands which fall under imperial rule, with the king's 127 provinces spanning from India to Ethiopia (1:1). They are transported to Persia, apparently without their consent (2:3, 8), and held captive in the king's harem until they receive a year of beauty treatments (2:12). After this process is over, they are taken to the king so that he can have (non-consensual) sex with them until he determines who best satisfies him sexually (2:4, 8). After Esther is chosen to replace Vashti as queen, the remaining girls are silenced and rendered invisible in the king's palace and also in the subsequent narrative. These elements of abduction, transportation, and captivity are all common stages in the criminal process of sex trafficking. Recognizing this process as it unfolds within the narrative exposes the inherent violence and horror of this biblical text.
>
> (2019, 34)

This violence and horror is not, however, evoked or alluded to in the teen girl Bibles that comment on the story of Esther. Instead, Esther's ordeal is framed as part of a divine plan to save the Jewish people from being killed during an imperial pogrom. In a *True Images* "Love Note" from God placed next to Esther 2–3, God tells his readers that, "Just as I chose Esther to be queen to save my people from certain death, so I have chosen you for a specific purpose. It may not be clear to you yet, but trust me. I am in control" (*TIB* 602). God is in control, and all's right with the world—even if you find yourself locked in a harem, waiting to be raped by a drunken, misogynistic king.

This theme of divine control comes up again in Esther's "Mirror Images" profile (*TIB* 609). Esther is described as a girl whom teen girls should emulate. "If God's never asked you to do something terrifying," readers are advised, "just be patient—he will!" By the strange logic of this statement, God wants teen girls to be "terrified" and girls must simply accept this. *True Images* editors fail to recognize the problematics of this statement, just as they do not see the gender violence writ large in this biblical text. Instead, Esther is described in this profile as having "lived a charmed life—winning the Miss Persia contest and marrying the king." Both *Revolve* (*RB* 572) and the *Bible for Teen Girls* (*BTG* 593, 600) likewise describe the king's quest for a new queen as a "beauty pageant." In *Revolve*'s introductory notes on the book of Esther, she is classed as "an absolutely gorgeous Jewish girl [who] wins [the king's] favour and gets the tiara" (*RB* 572). The *Bible for Teen Girls*, meanwhile, reimagines Esther's abuse as a romantic love story, describing her year-long compulsory beauty procedures as "spa treatments" that she received in order to "impress the king" and "win [his] heart" (*BTG* 593). And while this Bible admits that she was "probably still a teenager" when she was chosen to "go to the king's palace" (the term "harem" is not used here), there is not a hint of recognition that this is a sexually exploitative event (*BTG* 594).

To be fair, it is not only teen girl Bibles that frame the mass exploitation and rape depicted in Esther 2 as some sort of beauty contest; it is a relatively common interpretation in mainstream biblical scholarship (e.g. Fox 1991, 28; Duran 2004, 71). Yet this *is* a deeply problematic interpretation, which erases the violence embedded in the text. As Dunbar argues, "Defining the exploitation of the virgin girls as a 'beauty contest' ignores the elements of capture, captivity, and forced displacement which constitute trafficking and ultimately prevent the recognition of such experiences as exploitative" (2019, 35–36). The women and girls brought to the king's harem are far from voluntary participants in a pageant of any sort, but, as Dunbar insists, they are "victims of patriarchy and colonization, becoming the property of the empire, and with the exception of Esther, all disappear into the narrative world, never to be mentioned again" (2019, 36). This erasure of victims "enables sexual trafficking to survive and thrive, both in the biblical narrative and within contemporary contexts" (2019, 36).

While Esther's experience of sexual abuse is elided from these teen girl Bibles, her courage and obedience are nonetheless lauded. In the *True Images* "Mirror Images" profile of Esther, (titled "Gutsy Girl"), teen girl readers are encouraged to be "gutsy girls" themselves, brave enough to do things such as "refuse to give in to peer pressure" and to "boldly tell people you believe in Christ" (*TIB* 609). Most ironically, though, another example of being "gutsy" is having the courage to "hold onto your virginity," something that poor Esther couldn't manage, after being transported to a harem and raped by the Persian king. This *True Images* profile ignores the reality of sexual violence, suggesting implicitly that rape victims are not "gutsy" enough to avoid being raped.

The prophets

In the prophetic books of Hosea, Ezekiel, and Jeremiah, God's relationship with his covenant people Israel is sometimes spoken of using the metaphor of marriage (Hosea 1–3; Ezekiel 16, 23; Jeremiah 2:1–4:4). Within this metaphor, the Israelites are portrayed as God's unfaithful wife, who cuckolds her husband/deity with various "lovers" (foreign nations or other gods). God punishes his adulterous wife (variously identified as Israel, Jerusalem, and Samaria) with sexual and physical violence, to the point that she can do nothing else but submit, admit defeat, and return to her abusive spouse (e.g. Hosea 2:7). Once she is back, God reassures her that her sins are forgiven for now, and that the marriage will continue. The prophets use this metaphor to make the people understand the extent of their sins and the punishment they may expect from their angry, jealous God.

This prophetic marriage metaphor has been written about extensively in biblical scholarship, and feminist biblical interpreters have long noted its problematic linkage of intimate partner violence (IPV) to divine authority and punishment (see, for example, Brenner and van Dijk-Hemmes 1993, 165-93; Weems 1995; Magdalene 1995; Day 1999, 2000; Moughtin-Mumby 2008; Colgan 2018; Scholz 2010, 93–99, 179–208). To portray God as a violent, angry husband implies a divine sanction of IPV, or at least presents IPV as an appropriate (or even necessary) response to a wife's unfaithfulness, both in the biblical world and in contemporary culture (Day 1999, 176). The metaphorical wife of YHWH is variously trapped, starved, stoned, deprived of water, raped, cut with knives, publicly stripped and shamed, her property is destroyed, and she has her nose and ears cut off. Her voice is never heard, nor is she allowed to defend herself or deny the charges against her. Her all-powerful husband YHWH has declared her to be guilty, so who can argue that he is wrong, or that his punishments are undeserved? As Linda Day observes, within this marriage metaphor, "Female sexuality is not presented in its own right but only as an object for male possession, and physical abuse is insinuated to be necessary to keep women's sexuality under control" (1999, 176). This, continues Day, also reinforces patriarchal understandings of marriage, where women's bodies "are the property of men," and "if something does go awry in the relationship, it is the woman's fault" (1999, 176). Female readers of these prophetic texts are thus invited to read "against their own interests, to read them from a male perspective, to sympathise with the man and accept the woman's indictment as deserved" (Day 1999, 176). And this, notes Renita Weems, is deeply problematic, particularly for women who have themselves been victimized by IPV. What impact, she asks, does it have on women who "have been actually raped and battered, or who live daily with the threat of being raped and battered, to read sacred texts that justify rape and luxuriate obscenely in every detail of a woman's humiliation and battery?" (1995, 8).

While Jeremiah 2:1–4:4 and Ezekiel 23 receive no attention in the three teen girl Bibles I looked at, *True Images* includes two short editorial inserts which reference Ezekiel 16: a "Dare to Believe" note on Ezekiel 16:15 and a "Genuine Note" about Ezekiel 16:1–29 (both *TIB* 1121). These biblical verses list the sins of adulterous Jerusalem, but her punishments (stripping, shaming, rape, stoning, and cutting) are not outlined until later in the chapter (vv.35–42). Neither of the *True Images* notes mention these punishments; nor (unsurprisingly) do they reference the problematic nature of God's relationship with Jerusalem. God first discovered Jerusalem when she had been abandoned as an infant (v.6), and began a sexual relationship with her after she became "old enough for love" (v.8). *True Images* skips over this disturbing turn of events, and the editorial notes focus instead on girls' purity and faithfulness to God. In the "Genuine" note, Jerusalem is described as "beautiful and pure" on her wedding day, but she lost her purity chasing after false gods and other nations, "just as a prostitute has encounters with other men." This allusion to sex-workers is disquieting, as it implicitly equates them with "adulterous" women who deserve to be violently punished. The "Dare to Believe" note references Ezekiel 16:15 ("But you trusted in your beauty and used your fame to become a prostitute. You lavished your favors on anyone who passed by and your beauty became his") and reminds girl readers not to "trust in" their own gifts, but to reserve their trust for "the Giver." This a rather obtuse note, but again serves to reiterate the wrongfulness of Jerusalem's behaviour and to implicitly justify her punishments. It also implicitly undermines the value of girls' own strengths and abilities, a prominent theme in *True Images* that I will return to in Chapter 3.

The *Revolve* Bible also mentions Ezekiel 16, but like *True Images*, it completely ignores the violence God perpetrates against Jerusalem.

Instead, this text of terror is turned into a lesson about make-up and "beauty" (*RB* 985). God, we are told, chose the Israelite people "to be his own" and he "promised them blessings beyond their dreams, if they'd just stay close to him and do things his way." Clearly, the violence inflicted on Jerusalem is entirely her fault, because she failed to do things God's "way." Teen girl readers are then reminded that "True beauty isn't about hair and make-up"; they should not get "hung up" on their physical appearance but should remember that true beauty comes from their relationship with God. God's abusive and controlling relationship with Jerusalem in Ezekiel 16 is thus reframed as something "beautiful"; the implication here is that girls can only achieve "true beauty" if they too enter into a similarly controlling relationship with God (more of which in Chapter 3).

While the teen girl Bibles tend to spend minimal time on the marriage metaphor in Ezekiel and Jeremiah, they nonetheless lavish some attention on its appearance in the book of Hosea. Hosea 1–3 relates the prophet's own marriage to his unfaithful wife Gomer, which serves as a metaphor for God's covenant relationship with Israel. God instructs Hosea: "Go, take for yourself a wife of whoredom and have children of whoredom, for the land commits great whoredom by forsaking the Lord" (Hosea 1:2). Hosea follows God's instructions and marries a woman called Gomer, with whom he has three children. Gomer/Israel must then be punished for her unfaithfulness—she is stripped, deprived of water, starved, and held captive (2:1–13). Hosea/God then plans to "allure" his beaten-down wife, leading her into the wilderness and speaking "tenderly" to her (2:14), promising (or threatening?) that she will live with him for "many days" to come (3:3).

In *True Images*, the story of Hosea and Gomer is used to warn girls against the perils of spiritual and sexual unfaithfulness. The introductory notes for Hosea focus on the book's depiction of "adultery," which, we are told, "destroys everything in its path" (*TIB* 1191). Hosea is described as a man who "experienced the pain of adultery. God told Hosea to marry a woman who would be unfaithful to him. Hosea felt the terrible pain of dealing with an adulterous wife." The "terrible pain" experienced by Gomer through spousal violence is not mentioned here, or anywhere else in *True Images*. Her/Israel's decision to return to her abusive husband/God (because life with him is more bearable than the abuse she is currently enduring at his hands; Hosea 2:7) is reframed as evidence of Hosea's/God's benevolent forgiveness: "God told Hosea to go and bring his wife back and to love her again," these introductory notes tell us. "Why? Because that's exactly what God does for us! He brings us back and loves us, even though we hurt him deeply. Don't let anything ever keep you from running back into the loving arms of God." God's "loving arms" are the self-same arms that inflicted life-threatening punishment on his metaphorical wife; yet this is not mentioned. Instead, *True Images* sends a dangerous message to teen girl readers that IPV has divine sanction, and that women are always better off living with their abusers. This is bizarre, given that a *True Images* "In Focus" profile about family violence (*TIB* 336) explicitly states that "physical abuse is never okay with God. Your heavenly father wants you to be safe from harm … If someone is abusing you, it is not your fault, It is theirs. You have nothing to be ashamed of, and you definitely don't deserve it. No one does." No one, it seems, apart from unfaithful wives.

True Images' elision of IPV from Hosea 1–3 is likewise continued in Gomer's "Mirror Images" profile (*TIB* 1196). Teen girls are reminded that they can be "just like" Gomer—unfaithful to their God. Gomer's "sinfulness led her to a life of slavery, and it was Hosea's right to get rid of her for her adultery." Moreover, Hosea is identified as Gomer's saviour, rather than her abuser: he "brought her back from slavery, and then he lovingly invited her back into his home as his wife, treating her just as wonderfully as if she were his new, beautiful, virgin bride. After Gomer had treated him in cruel ways he didn't deserve, Hosea gave her mercy and grace she didn't deserve." Here, Gomer's suffering is attributed to her self-inflicted "slavery"—she is a sinner who does not deserve her husband's kindness and love—only a "beautiful, virgin bride" deserves those, it seems. Hosea's abusive actions are left unmentioned, he is rendered distant from her suffering (he got "rid" of her, her "slavery" takes her away from him), and his actions are justified and valorized.

This "Mirror Images" profile of Gomer adopts similar techniques to those commonly used in media reports of IPV, where victim blaming, perpetrator valorization, and passive voice help to blame the victim and minimize the perpetrator's culpability (Gilmore 2019, 106–22). Women's perceived wrongdoings are used to justify the violence enacted against them; news headlines report that unfaithful wives "drove" their poor husbands over the edge, and thus the violence that ensued was inevitable and deserved.[10] The "Good Guy trope" (Gilmore 2019, 111) is used time and again to remind us that men who murder, rape, and abuse their partners are really great blokes, and *they* are the ones who are suffering the most.[11] Other headlines tell us that women were "beaten," "slapped," "stabbed," and "murdered," but make no mention of the person who actually *did* these things, effectively erasing the perpetrator from their involvement in the crime.[12] As Jane Gilmore notes, invisible perpetrators impact "how we think about and understand violence"; when male violence is reported in the passive voice, "violent men are rendered invisible" and their acts of violence are likewise erased (2019, 110). But make no mistake. Gomer wasn't "led" to a "life of slavery" by her own "sinfulness"—Hosea physically assaulted and emotionally abused her.

Just as disturbingly, though, this "Mirror Images" profile wants teen girls to liken themselves to Gomer. Readers are reminded that their "sin" against God "is as hurtful as Gomer's sins were against Hosea ... an insult to our perfect God" (*TIB* 1196). If we follow this to its logical conclusion, then sinful girls deserve the same punishment meted out to Gomer. Readers are asked, "Like Gomer, do you struggle to remain faithful to following God? Does your attention wander to other people and other things? Is your heart divided between God and your own interests?" God demands girls' full attention—nothing else will do. And once again, the "Good Guy" trope is drawn on, as Hosea's treatment of Gomer is reframed as something magnificently benevolent: "The shocking thing about this story is not the audacity of Gomer's unfaithfulness. It's Hosea's persistence. Before and after Gomer's waywardness, Hosea's love remained." Sorry, but the *really* "shocking" thing about Hosea 1–3—and about this "Mirror Images" profile—is the way that both texts minimize and justify IPV by blaming the victims and heroizing the perpetrators. Teenage girls are effectively being told that women "deserve" violent abuse and control, and that they should "thank" and "praise" a God who mandates deadly gender violence. It's unconscionable.[13]

The *Revolve* Bible also includes a number of editorial notes on Gomer, which, like *True Images*, elide the violence she endured and cast her as a wanton woman undeserving of Hosea's love. In the introductory notes to the book, readers are told that Gomer "had a very bad reputation—her phone number would have been plastered all over the boys' locker room" (*RB* 1052). God created this "good-guy/bad-girl setup to give his people a living example of his saving relationship with them." Abusive husbands exemplify "good guys," it appears, while sexually agentic and horribly abused wives become archetypal "bad girls." These introductory notes describe Gomer's life as being "in a downward spiral of sin, including adultery, leaving her family, and prostitution." Playing fast and loose with the Hosea 3 text, the editors tell us with voyeuristic relish that Gomer was being auctioned off at a slave market before Hosea rescued her, "and from what history says about slavery at that time, Gomer probably stood naked so that interested buyers could examine the 'merchandise'." There is nothing in Hosea 3 about Gomer being at a "slave market," and the only mention of her being naked is when she/Israel is "stripped" by her abusive husband/God (Hosea 2:3, 10). Yet in these introductory notes, Hosea's/God's perpetration of the abuse is again elided, and Gomer is blamed for it herself. Readers are invited to imagine Gomer naked and humiliated, and to recognize her nakedness as a sign of her guilt and shame; meanwhile, Hosea's determination to retain control of his errant wife is reframed as a "powerful picture" of "a husband's forgiveness."

Indeed, Gomer's "Ladies of the Bible" profile in *Revolve* accentuates her abject sinfulness even further. Using more creative licence, editors tell us that she "sold herself into slavery and works as a prostitute. Her owner keeps her busy with many men ... Though she's married with kids, she's had many lovers" (*RB* 1060). These "lovers" mistreat her and the work is "humiliating," but she "liked chasing after new lovers." Gomer thus becomes a masochistic sex slave, complicit in her own abuse and humiliation at the hands of the many men who are raping her. Hosea, we are told, "had been kind" to her; clearly, we are meant to forget that he stripped, starved, and entrapped her (although ironically, this profile tells us that Gomer looks "tired and thin"). *Revolve* editors seem intent on shifting the blame for Hosea's crimes against Gomer onto her anonymous "lovers." And Hosea's "kindness" is reiterated in a "Daily Devos" note, which interprets Hosea 3:1–2 as proof that "love conquers all" (*RB* 1056).

As in *True Images*, readers of *Revolve* are asked to liken themselves to Gomer. A "Daily Devos" note on Hosea 2:23 tells teen girls that "we aren't that different from Gomer or the nation of Israel" (*RB* 1054). Before readers start to panic about the abuse that lies in store for them, they are reassured that "God wants to show us mercy." Again, the "wooing" language of Hosea 2:21–23 is seen as a wonderful sign of God's mercy, rather than the coercive tactics of a serial abuser, who offers his victim just enough affection to stop her leaving for good. In another "Daily Devos" note on Hosea 3:1–3 (*RB* 1056), Hosea's "buying back" Gomer from her new husband is linked to God "buying" teen girl readers through the salvation offered by Jesus' death, so that they now "belong" to God. Hosea's purchase of Gomer ought to remind us "of what God went through to rescue us from our sin." Despite the use of "us," it is teen girls specifically who are being addressed here (*Revolve* is a teen girl Bible, after all), and they are being invited to liken themselves to an abused woman who should show gratitude to her violent husband for his refusal to leave her alone.

The *Bible for Teen Girls* has far less to say about Gomer, but it does include a short study note on Hosea 2:19 (*BTG* 1092), which the NIV translates as, "I will betroth you to me forever, I will betroth you in righteousness and justice, in love and compassion." As with *True Images*, the violence Hosea perpetrates against Gomer is not mentioned in this note, other than to say that the book of Hosea "isn't easy to read." Instead, it highlights Gomer's sin of promiscuity—she is "adulterous" and a "prostitute." It also mentions that Hosea pays Gomer's lover "the price of a female slave" to buy her back (Hosea 3:1–2), as though this were a somewhat laudable gesture. Gomer is effectively bought and sold by these two men as though she were a piece of property and is given no choice about whom she marries (if anyone). Yet this is not mentioned either, and readers are simply reminded yet again of Hosea's tireless love for his unfaithful wife and God's "intense passion for his people"—a passion that seems to require violence to sustain it.

A final note about gender violence in the prophetic texts: Isaiah 3:16–24 steps away from the marriage metaphor but teen girl Bible editors clearly consider it a useful teaching tool to reinforce their evangelical purity rhetoric. In this passage, the prophet Isaiah mentions the "haughty" women of Zion, who walk the streets "with outstretched necks, flirting with their eyes, strutting along with swaying hips, with ornaments jingling on their ankles" (v.16; NIV).[14] God warns that he will punish and shame these women, inflicting them with sores, making their hair fall out, and stripping them of their robes and finery (vv.18–24). *Revolve* uses this passage to remind teen girl readers not to flirt and "lead guys on" by dressing "super-sexy" or putting on "a ton of make-up" (*RB* 798). Similarly, *True Images* references these verses to warn teen girls that, while God does not mind them having new clothes, jewellery, or nice hairstyles, he punishes the women in the text because they are "vain and conceited and self-centred. They cared more about their appearance than about honoring God. And because God refuses to take second place, he said he would strip them of the finery they were so proud of so they would turn to him instead" (*TIB* 892). Stripping and shaming women is perfectly acceptable, it seems, if they fail to put God first. Both *True Images* and *Revolve* thus equate teenage girls with the "promiscuous," "vain," and "sinful" women evoked in the biblical texts. Time and again, girls are reminded that they too are prone to sinfulness, that they are utterly dependent on God, and that God demands their unwavering love and loyalty—or else. To be honest, it is exhausting to read, and I can only imagine how teen girls feel about themselves when *they* read these editorial notes. Not too good, I suspect.

The sound of silence: other biblical texts depicting rape

The sections above list biblical texts depicting sexual violence that are discussed in the three teen girl Bibles I studied. Other biblical texts that likewise portray rape and sexual assault receive no such editorial treatment. Many of these biblical texts present sexually violent acts as a "normal" or even desirable part of Israelite life. As with the rapes of Hagar, Zilpah, Bilhah, and Bathsheba (mentioned earlier), the coercive and violent nature of these acts are unacknowledged by the biblical authors. Lot's two daughters rape him in order to become pregnant and continue the family line (Genesis 19:30–38).[15] Biblical slave owners have sex with their slaves, which, as we noted in our discussion of Genesis 16 and 30, is tantamount to rape, given that slaves were unable to grant or withhold their consent (e.g. Leviticus 19:20–22; Matthew 8:5–13 // Luke 7:1–10).[16] Fathers can seemingly offer their daughters to angry mobs of men, particularly when their male guests are being threatened with gang rape (Genesis 19:8; Judges 19:22). Sexual violence during warfare is also taken for granted, and is perpetrated by Israel with impunity (e.g. Genesis 34:29; Numbers 25:6–8; 31:18; Judges 21:10–23); there is even a Deuteronomic law that grants divine sanction to this practice (Deuteronomy 21:10–14). And while some allusions to wartime rape are used to arouse readers' pity (e.g. Lamentations 1:8–10; 5:11) or to send a divine warning of terrible times ahead (e.g. Jeremiah 38:23; Zechariah 14:2), rape remains "part of the furniture" of war, something that is presented as "permissible, advantageous, and as divinely mandated" (Stiebert 2019, 28).

Metaphorical sexual violence is also used in the prophetic and apocalyptic traditions. In addition to the marriage metaphor texts I discussed above, God is depicted using sexually aggressive tactics to punish Israel's personified enemies as well as personified Israel herself. Isaiah 47 describes the shame that will befall the "virgin daughter of Babylon," whose arrogance and sinfulness will be punished by God through her stripping and shaming (Isaiah 47:2–3).[17] In Jeremiah 13:22, Jerusalem's "many sins" lead to her skirts being "torn off" and her "body mistreated" (another fine example of invisible perpetrator language here). And in the apocalyptic text of Revelation 2:22, God threatens to cast the "false prophetess" Jezebel "on a bed of suffering," a phrase, which Johanna Stiebert rightly notes, has "ominous overtones of sexual violence" (2019, 30). Revelation 17 also describes the "great harlot" Babylon, who will eventually be attacked by the beast that she rides; this beast will "bring her to ruin and leave her naked … eat her flesh and burn her with fire" (v.16). Once again, God is the orchestrator of this female figure's sexual violation (Stiebert 2019, 30–31).

Elsewhere in the Bible, however, rape is presented explicitly as something sinful, unlawful, or at least a slightly underhand means of power play between men. Absalom publicly rapes his father David's unnamed concubines in order to assert his dominance over the king and bolster his persistent claims to the crown (2 Samuel 15:13–16; 16:20–23; 20:3). Reuben's rape of Bilhah is met with his father Jacob's disapproval, but only because she is Jacob's sexual property (Genesis 35:22; 49:3–4)—her response and her feelings are not even documented (see Scholz 2010, 72, 75). Earlier in Genesis, in a tradition that closely parallels Judges 19, the men of Sodom attempt to rape Lot's two heavenly visitors, which seals the divine destruction of Sodom and Gomorrah (Genesis 19). Meanwhile, in the Deuteronomic law codes, the rape of an unbetrothed virgin is treated as a property violation (against the girl's father), and the rapist must pay him a monetary fine and marry the girl without recourse to divorce (Deuteronomy 22:28–29). If the woman is betrothed, and rape can be proven,[18] the perpetrator is put to death, but the woman is declared innocent of the capital crime of adultery (Deuteronomy 22:25–26). The important point here is that a woman's rape is viewed in these biblical traditions as a crime against her male "owner," rather than against *her*.

As I noted at the start of this chapter, there is a great deal of sexual violence depicted in the Bible. Yet not all of it is recognized as rape. When biblical interpreters and readers likewise fail to recognize it, they help to keep it under wraps and thus become complicit (perhaps unwittingly) in reinscribing the silence that surrounds sexual violence, not only in the biblical texts themselves but in contemporary culture too. By ignoring the violence and coercion in biblical stories of rape, and the way that these stories silence rape victims, readers only serve to sanction these texts' apparent indifference to, ignorance of, or even approval of sexual violence.[19] And this, in turn, has a significant impact on how we respond to and understand rape today. When we accept biblical texts' erasure of sexual violence, and its silencing of biblical rape victims, we send a potent message to Bible-reading communities (and others too) that rape does not really matter, and that its victims don't deserve to be heard. We also allow rape myths, which are embedded in these biblical texts and their interpretations, to flourish unchecked. As Stiebert notes, "Because the Bible continues to exert influence into the present, erasure of rape from the Bible can enable the easier perpetuation of rape myths … [which] have bearing and a damaging impact on real lives" (2019, 7). The teen girl Bibles I discuss in this book, which include copious editorial commentaries on the biblical texts, perpetuate rape myths through what they *say* about biblical gender violence, but also by what they *don't* say. These Bibles' constant failure to recognize rape in the sacred texts, and their unwillingness to talk honestly about this topic with their teen girl readers, only sustains the silence, shame, and victim blame that surrounds this pervasive crime, leaving it to continue unremarked and downplaying its devastating consequences.

It's such a shame: victim blaming and the erasure of sexual violence

The failure of teen girl Bibles to recognize biblical sexual violence is also mirrored in their discussions of contemporary teen girls' sexual experiences. On more than one occasion, the editorial sections in some of these Bibles describe a form of abusive sexual behaviour, which they problematize because of its *purity* implications, rather than its coercive nature. As a result, the violence inherent in these sexual acts is minimized or ignored, and the victims are blamed, stigmatized, and shamed. This shame is highly encoded for gender, with girls' sexual experiences being held up for far more scrutiny and critique than boys', whether or not these experiences are consensual or coerced.

Let me offer a few examples from *True Images*. In an "In Focus" profile on sexting, the fictional figure of Bianca tells readers that her boyfriend Sebastian pressured her into sending him a photo of her bare breast (*TIB* 543). She admits that she was "so scared of getting caught," but Sebastian reassured her that he wouldn't tell anyone. After Bianca sends him the photo, "he sent me a *bunch* of texts that made me uncomfortable" (emphasis original), presumably because they were sexually explicit. The following day at school, Sebastian's phone is confiscated by staff after some misdemeanour, the picture is found, and Bianca's parents are called in by the school's assistant principal. "They were so angry," Bianca admits, "They didn't understand why I would send a picture like that. They made me break up with Sebastian, and now he is mad at me too. I am so scared he will show the picture to everyone now."

This profile is problematic on a number of counts. Bianca makes clear that she is pressured into sexting with Sebastian—she is "scared" by her boyfriend's initial request and made to feel "uncomfortable" by the unsolicited sexts that he subsequently sends her (*TIB* 543). It is obvious that she does not feel as though she has the agency or choice to refuse his requests. Yet despite this, her parents are "angry" with *her* when the photo is found, rather than directing their anger at Sebastian, or checking to see if she has been victimized or pressured into sending the photo in the first place. And now she has to live with the permanent fear that Sebastian will get his revenge by showing the picture to others.

The editorial response to Bianca's story does little to ease her shame or fear. The tone is authoritative and removed, as though the editors wish to distance themselves from this sordid teenage tale. Sexting, they tell us, "is not harmless fun" and risks "exposure and public shaming" for everyone involved, including, we presume, girls like Bianca who are pressured into doing it (*TIB* 543). This will be cold comfort for any teen girl readers currently sharing Bianca's plight.

More disturbingly, though, the editors continue with another warning: "if you are underage, [sexting] is illegal and can be prosecuted under the law. It is considered child pornography. A single text or photo can *get you or the recipient into real trouble*" (*TIB* 543; emphasis added). Now let me be clear here. US federal law defines "child pornography" as "any visual depiction of sexually explicit conduct involving a minor (someone under 18 years of age)" (Department of Justice 2020).[20] The "production, distribution, reception, and possession of an image of child pornography" is prohibited under this law, and it is illegal "to persuade, induce, entice, or coerce a minor to engage in sexually explicit conduct for purposes of producing visual depictions of that conduct" (Department of Justice 2020). Nowhere does this law state that the minor involved will be held liable or culpable for *any* complicity in this crime. Yet the *True Images* editors seem to suggest this in the way they frame their discussion. They do not clarify *who* can face prosecution for "child pornography," but the statement that a photo can "get you or the recipient into real trouble" suggests that underage girls themselves could in fact be prosecuted. There is no mention here that any person who tries to procure a picture of an underage girl is sexually victimizing her, not to mention breaking the law. There is no attempt to deal with the very real and very pervasive occurrence of child sexual victimization ("child pornography") in the United States and beyond. There is no effort made to offer teen girls practical advice about resisting or reporting unwanted requests for sexually explicit images and sexts (other than the pretty useless "Just say no" advice that's given). There is no acknowledgment of the enormous emotional trauma faced by young people who are victimized by this crime. And while teen girl readers are told to report anyone who is pressuring them or bullying them into sexting, this coercive behaviour is described merely as "harassment," not a criminal act of sexualized violence or sexual victimization.

Of course, the advice at the end of Bianca's *True Images* profile takes us back to purity. "Sexting compromises your purity," readers are told, "and your purity is important to God—and to you. Stay safe by staying on the path of purity" (*TIB* 543). Teen girls' "safety" is contingent on their staying "pure." Girls who do find themselves in "unsafe" situations are clearly not being pure enough. Again, the sexual abuse and coercion inherent in non-consensual sexting is utterly elided; instead, it is simply assumed that girls always have the agency and ability to control their own sexuality—sexual coercion and victimization are completely unacknowledged. Moreover, there is no distinction made between girls who happily and consensually sext with their partner and those who are being sexually victimized through this activity. There is no effort to address Bianca's (and countless real teen girls') fears that their sexts will be shared by resentful ex-boyfriends. And any girl who does sext—or has been pressured or threatened into doing so—must go to sleep at night knowing that she is no longer deemed pleasing or "pure" in the eyes of her evangelical God.

True Images also has an "In Focus" profile on abusive relationships. Titled "Don't Leave Me Lonely" (*TIB* 1021), it relates the story of Paige, who admits that she's "always had a guy" in her life, and her best friends tease her that she's never without a boyfriend. Paige frets that this could mean she has a "dependency problem," but more pressingly, she worries about her current boyfriend Austin, whom she's "scared *not* to be with" because "he'd go nuts" (emphasis original). Paige tried to break up with Austin, but "he freaked out" on her, calling her and threatening to harm himself if they didn't get back together. He also drove past her house all night, calling her repeatedly. But because he was "so sweet" the next day, apologizing for his behaviour, Paige decided to stay with him. "Sometimes I'm still not sure he's right for me," she admits, "But without him I'd be alone."

This heart-breaking story will be all too familiar to many girls and women. Austin is emotionally abusing Paige, make no mistake, manipulating and controlling her emotionally using threats and harassment. The *True Images* editorial response to Paige certainly points this out, for which we should be thankful. Yet it also blames her too.[21] "If you're constantly in relationships," it states, "*choosing* guys that are controlling or emotionally abusive, or *putting up with* abusive behavior from a guy, you are in an unhealthy pattern. These are signs of dependency and self-esteem issues" (emphasis added). Again, to be clear, girls *do not* "choose" controlling and abusive guys; coercive control and emotional abuse are never at the top of girls' "things to look for in the perfect boyfriend" list. And no one "puts up" with a partner's abusive behaviour, as though it's a mildly bad habit, like being late for dates or leaving the toilet seat up. As I discuss in the following chapter, victims of intimate partner abuse are coerced and controlled by their abuser, which compromises their ability to escape their victimization. Yet *True Images* does not acknowledge this, because it is too busy blaming girls like Paige for their "overreliance" on boyfriends. Teen girls are advised to get some help from a counsellor "to help you figure out *why you're drawn to unhealthy relationships*" (emphasis added), again implicating girls in their own emotional abuse. There is no condemnation of the abusive boyfriend's behaviour; no recognition that girls may lack the agency to escape emotional abuse, especially when their sense of autonomy has been so undermined by their abuser; and no consideration of the various traumas or inequities that might render a teenage girl particularly vulnerable to the attentions of an abusive partner. And while this profile reminds girls to "act *now*" if a boyfriend threatens them or "actually physically hurts" them (emphasis original),[22] this is all too little too late. Emotional abuse and coercive control do untold damage to girls and women, yet here in *True Images*, they are trivialized as problems that can be blamed on the neediness and poor choices of the teen girls themselves. Again, this is unconscionable. Any form of abuse and coercive control is never the victim's fault. Let me repeat, it is *never* their fault.

There is something else that needs repeating—girls do *not* have to put up with sexual abuse (or abuse in any form). A truism perhaps, but worth passing on to the editors of *Revolve*, who offer readers a disquieting "Daily Devos" note based on the book of Esther. The note reminds girls that God is always with them, even during the worst of times, just as he was with Esther. It lists various personal problems that girls may face, including their parents divorcing, their own ill-health, and the possibility that they have "endured some kind of abuse" (*RB* 581). It then suggests that girls have "just got to hang with it and have faith because God isn't ever going to allow evil things to win! Things may start out bad, but God will only let it go on as long as absolutely necessary to make things work out for the very best" (581). Abuse is thus framed as something girls have to tolerate, consent to, or "hang with," because it is part of a divine plan—something that is ultimately advantageous to their lives. Similar messages are repeated elsewhere in *Revolve*—bad things happen, but girls need to tolerate them with fortitude, knowing that God is doing it "for the very best" of reasons.

When I first read this "Daily Devos" note, I had to walk away from my desk for a moment and take several deep breaths. Because it is so very, very wrong. *Revolve* editors *should* be telling their teen girl readers that they *never*, under *any* circumstances, have to "hang with" their abuse—sexual or otherwise—or accept that it is in any way "good" for them. Like other teen girl Bibles, though, *Revolve* is so intent on perpetuating evangelical Christian ideals of female passivity and subordination that it is prepared to instruct teenage girls to be complicit in their own victimization. And that is reprehensible.

Conclusion

Episodes of sexual violence depicted in the biblical texts are not always acknowledged in evangelical teen girl Bibles. Rape, coercive control, and intimate partner violence are regularly erased, or reframed as a punishment for a woman's sexual sins. And even when sexual violence *is* recognized in the editorial notes included in these Bibles, problems still persist. Victim blaming remains prominent, as does the elision of the perpetrator. And the incessant focus on sexual purity heightens the stakes for sexually abused girls. While these Bibles may encourage their teen readers to disclose sexual assault or abuse, it is painful to imagine the repercussions of them doing so if they belong to a purity-pushing evangelical culture, which measures a girl's spiritual worthiness according to her sexual "purity." Sexual violence is so often silenced in faith communities and churches; as sex is framed in the rhetoric of sin, there is a reluctance to talk about it, or to offer young people (particularly unmarried people) advice about consent, sexual violence prevention, and healthy sexual relationships. Girls and women who are impacted by sexual violence are therefore often reluctant to turn to their churches for support, particularly if they suspect that they will be blamed themselves (Klein 2019, ch. 4).

While some of the teen girl Bibles I looked at do offer the contact details for national rape crisis and sexual abuse helplines, I worry that they also all encourage victims to talk to someone within their own evangelical circles—a parent, counsellor, or trusted (Christian) adult, who will likely be equally well versed in the church's purity discourse. First responses to disclosures of sexual harm are vitally important in shaping the victim's experiences of help-seeking and their subsequent journey towards recovery. If teenage girls are faced by further blame, shame, and stigma when they do disclose their abuse, this may be experienced as a "second assault," which could have devastating consequences for their emotional, psychological, and spiritual wellbeing

(Koon-Magnin and Schulze 2019; see also Vagianos 2017). As Klein argues, "The way in which [the evangelical community] wrongfully classifies sexual violence … can re-traumatize survivors, making the church—a place that many would hope to be a safe haven—a very dangerous place for survivors" (2019, Ch. 13, Kindle).

Shame on you, teen girl Bibles, shame on you.

Notes

1 For a concise but thorough overview of sexual violence in the Bible, see Stiebert (2019, 19–32).
2 In Genesis 16, Sarah is still known by her original name Sarai, while Abraham is Abram; God gives them their new names in Genesis 17 (vv. 5 and 15). To avoid confusion, I use "Abraham" and "Sarah" when discussing both Genesis 16 and 21.
3 See Junior (2019, 101–25) for further discussion of these and other interpretations that draw connections between Hagar and women of colour.
4 None of the teen girl Bibles I looked at include any editorial discussion about Abraham's dismissal of Hagar and Ishmael (Genesis 21). Yet this too is a violent act, where a woman and her son are driven into the desert, essentially to die. It is another example of the ways in which these Bibles silence and erase the patriarchal abuse of women.
5 "When Shechem, son of Hamor the Hivite, the ruler of that area, saw her, he took her and raped her" (Genesis 34:2, NIV). The NCV translation says that Shechem "forced [Dinah] to have sexual relations with him." For further discussion on the interpretation of this verse as a depiction of sexual violence, see Blyth (2010, 38–92); Scholz (2010, 32–38); Stiebert (2019, 25–26).
6 See Blyth (2010, 158–93) for an overview of interpretive traditions that blame Dinah for her rape.
7 Detailed analysis of the sexual violence in Judges 19–21 can be found in Paynter (2020); Harding (2019); Exum (2016, 140–62); Scholz (2010, 135–55).
8 For further discussion of Bathsheba as a victim of rape, see Exum (2016, 135–62); Scholz (2010, 99–103).
9 It is worth noting, though, that Bathsheba's "Mirror Images" profile is listed under the subject title "Rape" in the *True Images* index. In evangelical purity literature, this is far from a consensus view. For example, Gresh talks about Bathsheba's "sin" of letting herself carelessly be seen by David while she was bathing (2011, ch. 6, Kindle). Gresh also raises the possibility that Bathsheba may have "desired spectators" and deliberately shown her body to the king (2011, ch. 6, Kindle).
10 Gilmore offers many examples of this in real news headlines she has collected over the years, including "Man Killed Wife over Lesbian Affair and Small Penis Taunts, Court Hears" (2019, 119).
11 For example, Gilmore cites Australia's *Courier Mail*, which reported a story about a man charged with three breaches of domestic violence restraining orders, using the headline "Man in Court after Losing His Wife, His House, His Job" (Gilmore 2020). With regard to the "Good Guy"

trope, Gilmore describes a case from 2017, where a man who shot his wife in front of their children was described on every major news outlet in the state of Victoria as "good," "nice," and "decent" (2019, 111–12).
12 One example Gilmore offers is "Woman Dies in Hospital after Stabbing Attack in NSW" (2019, 109).
13 Emily Colgan (2018) interrogates a similarly troubling reading of Hosea 1–3 presented by John and Stasi Eldredge in their best-selling Christian self-help book for women, *Captivating: Unveiling the Mystery of a Woman's Soul* (2005).
14 The NCV translates Isaiah 3:16 as follows: "The women of Jerusalem are proud. They walk around with their heads held high, and they flirt with their eyes. They take quick, short steps, making noise with their ankle bracelets."
15 It is unclear from the text whether or not the narrator approves of the daughters' actions. Lot is unaware of what happens, as the women ensure he is intoxicated first (Genesis 19:32). This detail may be included to exonerate him from blame, or reduce his complicity in these incestuous deeds, which is ironic given that intoxicated *women* are regularly blamed in contemporary culture for their own sexual assaults.
16 For further discussion of the coercive relationship between the centurion and his slave (Matthew 8:5-13 // Luke 7:1-10), see Zeichmann (2018).
17 Stripping and exposing was clearly a potent means of humiliating one's enemies in the biblical world; in 2 Samuel 10:1–4, David sent a delegation to the Ammonite king Hanun, ostensibly to pass on his sympathies for Hanun's father's death. Hanun, however, suspected these envoys were there to spy out the land, so he seized them, shaved off half of each man's beard, and "cut off their garments at the buttocks," before sending them on their way (v.4, NIV). The men, we learn, were "greatly humiliated" (v.5).
18 In Deuteronomy 22:25–27, the veracity of a woman's accusation of rape is decided by the location of the alleged assault. If it happened in the countryside, then she is deemed to be telling the truth, as no one would have heard her cry for help (vv.25–26). But if she claims she was raped in the city, then it is assumed that she is lying (because someone would have heard her cries), and she faces capital punishment as an adulteress (v.27). The flawed logic of this law is easy to see: just because a woman does not call for help when she is being raped does not mean that the sexual act was consensual. Yet this same misperception persists today, and continues to influence how "believable" a woman's accusations are in the eyes of her family and community, law enforcement, jurors, and the media. See Rape Crisis (2020) for an overview of the many different and common victim responses during their assault, including "freezing" and "flopping," where the victim remains still and silent as an instinctive survival response.
19 For further discussion about the elision of rape from biblical interpretation, and the unwillingness of some biblical scholars to identify rape in biblical texts, see Stiebert (2019, 4–8); Scholz (2005).
20 In the United Kingdom, the phrase "child pornography" is not used, and the laws refer to "Indecent and Prohibited Images of Children" (Crown Prosecution Service 2020). Although a bona fide US legal term, "child pornography" is deeply problematic, as it "likens online child abuse

material to an acceptable sub-genre of mainstream, adult, consensual pornography ... [rather than] the photographic or video evidence of a criminal act against infants, children and young people" that "contributes to the normalisation of child sexual assault" (Liddell and Powell 2015). I focus on US legislation above (and use the term "child pornography," albeit in scare quotes) because *True Images* also uses this term, being published in the United States.
21 And, as I discuss in the next chapter, this "In Focus" profile is especially ironic, given that God is presented in *True Images* as a particularly manipulative and coercively controlling presence in teen girls' lives.
22 The inclusion of the word "actually" here rankles me; grammatically unnecessary, it implicitly suggests that there will be occasions when teen girls will not "actually" be physically hurt by a partner, even if they claim to have been.

3 Christian complementarianism and coercive control in teen girl Bibles

In this chapter, I argue that the notes, profiles, and devotionals included in two of my teen girl Bibles—*True Images* and *Revolve*—reinforce complementarian discourses of female subordination by (unwittingly, perhaps) mirroring tactics used by perpetrators of coercive control. Teen girl readers of these two Bibles are threatened, degraded, gaslighted, surveilled, microregulated, stalked, love-bombed, isolated, and utterly intimidated into conforming to the evangelical ideal of teenage girlhood: compliant, subordinated, and silenced. They are continually told that the best relationship they can have (or rather, *must* have) with God demands their total subordination and obedience. Male authority and female subservience are thus normalized both within and beyond divine-human relationships, and the control of teen girls' bodies and lives by a male-identified deity (and male authority figures more generally) is framed as both desirable and sacred. This, I contend, helps to sustain religious and social discourses that make girls and women continually vulnerable to multiple forms of violence.

Complementarianism

To understand how tactics of coercive control are operating in these teen girl Bibles, let me first map out the principles that underpin Christian complementarianism.[1] This doctrine is encoded with strict gender expectations, based on the belief that God created two distinct genders (male and female), who both have equal value in God's eyes, but to whom God has given distinct roles and responsibilities. Complementarianism (also known as the "doctrine of submission," see Marsden 2018) insists that men and women must conform to different expectations around how they behave, think, and look. Men hold a God-given authority and power in their marital and family relationships, and women, in turn, must respect men's authority and help it to flourish. As Klein explains, "The man is to be undeniably masculine, even as he practices patience and understanding as a leader, whereas the woman is to be irrefutably feminine and to lovingly consent to and support the leadership of the man" (2018, ch. 2, Kindle; see also Marsden 2018, 75). Together, men and women can make a perfect whole, but, if either side strays from their divinely ordained roles, they risk damaging the stability and spiritual welfare of the family, church, and society (Marsden 2018, 75).

Complementarianism is by no means a benign ideology of gender. Rooted in patriarchy, it validates gender inequality and justifies women's subordination as a divine imperative. Men's control and domination of their wives is given scriptural sanction, while girls and women are taught to be submissive and to accept without question men's authority and leadership (Klein 2018, ch. 2, Kindle). Given this power imbalance, complementarian gender roles serve to justify and even sanctify abusive gender relationships and intimate partner violence (IPV) (Nason-Clark 1997, 1999; Klein 2018, ch. 2, Kindle). IPV becomes framed as another way for men to maintain their control over women and to punish them for challenging men's God-given authority. Subordinated women are also easier for men to control and commit violence against; indeed, IPV is scaffolded by perpetrators' power and control over their victims.[2] In other words, violence serves to perpetuate women's subordination and is also a *consequence* of their subordination (United Nations 2006, 28–30; cited in Marsden 2018, 74). This strong correlation between IPV and the rigid gender roles endorsed by complementarian doctrine has been established for decades. Yet, as Klein notes, the evangelical church rarely admits this relationship, preferring to preserve their commitment to this doctrine through "denial, minimization, and spiritualization of the abusive situation" (Klein 2018, ch. 2, Kindle). Or, to use Nancy Nason-Clark's evocative phrase (1999), the evangelical Christian church protects and preserves a "holy hush" around spousal abuse and IPV.

Complementarianism does not only foster *physical* abuse in Christian relationships. It is also horribly effective in sustaining and justifying emotional abuse too, including coercive control. Sharon Hayes and Samantha Jeffries define coercive control as "a pattern of intentional tactics employed by perpetrators with the intent of governing a woman's thoughts, beliefs or conduct and/or to punish them for resisting their regulation" (2015, 13).[3] These tactics are designed to bend the victim's will to that of the perpetrator, by inciting her sense of fear and entrapment. This allows the perpetrator to maintain his power and control in the relationship, while the victim becomes convinced that she cannot escape the abuse (Hayes and Jeffries 2015, 22, 28). As Hayes and Jeffries suggest, "The perpetrator is an individual intent on pursuing their own agenda, which is to train their women to be whatever they want her to be and be only what they want her to be, all the time" (2015, 28–29). Through their repeated experiences of fear, correction, humiliation, surveillance, and the threat of punishment, victims lose any sense of their own autonomy, as their victimizer attempts to control their thoughts, microregulate their everyday lives and activities, and redefine their reality. Scaffolded by patriarchal power structures, coercive control thus serves to legitimize male privilege and men's right to subordinate and dominate women (Hayes and Jeffries 2015, 23; Stark, 2007, 5). As Evan Stark explains, coercive control:

> is designed to stifle and co-opt women's gains, foreclosing negotiation over the organization, extent, and substance of women's activities in and around the home; obstruct their access to support; close the spaces in which they can reflect critically on their lives; and reimpose obsolete forms of dependence and personal service by micromanaging the enactment of stereotypic gender roles through "sexism with a vengeance."
>
> (2007, 194)

Stark goes on to note that men who perpetrate coercive control do so in order to "defend their traditional prerogatives against the perceived threats posed by women's increasing economic independence, cultural autonomy, and political/legal equality" (2007, 96). These "traditional prerogatives" of male power and authority lie at the heart of evangelical Christian complementarianism; coercive control may therefore be utilized (knowingly or not) within evangelical communities to prevent female members from embracing contemporary discourses of women's equity, agency, and autonomy.

Mapping the tactics of coercive control through teen girl Bibles

Perpetrators of coercive control employ a range of tactics to subordinate and control their victims, instilling in them a sense of fear and entrapment that prevents them from escaping the abusive relationship. Below, I list many of these tactics, defining them in more detail, then illustrating their articulation in the various editorial notes included in *True Images* and *Revolve*. I am sure the editors of these Bibles did not actively set out to do this, but they have succeeded nonetheless, perhaps because this coercive rhetoric is so pervasive and taken-for-granted in evangelical Christianity. Yet couched within the pages of a Bible, it is particularly effective. As Lisa Aronson Fontes notes, people with "special status" and authority (such as police officers, teachers, and employers) are often particularly adept at enacting coercive control (2015, 47). Their already established superior power allows them to deliberately lead a less powerful person "into a highly imbalanced relationship" that is "ripe for coercive control" (Fontes 2015, 47). In *True Images* and *Revolve*, such a "highly imbalanced relationship" is set up between God and teenage girls, and girls are regularly reminded of God's superior power, authority, and omnipotence. Wrapped as it is in the Christian language of love and obedience to God, we might be tempted to dismiss this rhetoric as a harmless religious discourse that encourages teen girls' devotion and loyalty to the deity. But it's not harmless, it's malignant; because it tells teen girls *time and again* that God wants them to be compliant, submissive, and controlled. And given that this message is situated (quite literally) within the pages of sacred scripture, it is imbued with an authority and sacredness that makes it far harder to dispute.

"If you're never punished, your brat-potential could skyrocket": threats, intimidation, and demands for obedience

Perpetrators of coercive control often use verbal threats, threatening behaviours, and intimidation to instil fear, shame, and anxiety in their victim (Hayes and Jeffries 2015, 29). These may include threats of violence (to the victim, her children, or her pets), emotional punishment (such as the withdrawal of affection, or the perpetrator threatening to harm *himself*), or public shaming (including threats to share the victim's intimate secrets or photographs with friends, family, or her employers). Through such threats and intimidation, the perpetrator can establish his "ownership" of the victim, subordinating her, ensuring her obedience, and reinforcing his authority and superior power (Fontes 2015, 50). This, in turn, can foster a victim's sense of her own unworthiness of better treatment, her dependence on her abuser, and her compliance and loyalty to him (Fontes 2015, 50; Stark 2007, 250). The perpetrator may also intimidate her more implicitly, by invading her personal life and her emotional world, claiming to know her every action and thought (more of which in a later section). This can have a devastating impact on the women and girls affected, shattering their psychological and emotional wellbeing and tying them more tightly to their abuser (Stark 2007, 250). Victims may experience feelings of anxiety and hopelessness, reinforcing their fears that they are unable to escape this relationship, as well as preventing them from seeking outside help (Hill 2019, ch.1, iBook).

In the *True Images* Bible, verbal threats and intimidation abound, with God cast as the perpetrator and teen girl readers his victims. Girls are warned repeatedly that if they disobey God, the consequences will be dire: "you'll end up paying for it sooner or later" (*TIB* 226); "you'll eventually find yourself in a painful predicament" (*TIB* 563); "God might just let you fall on your face" (699); "You'll pay for it when you do things your way instead of God's" (*TIB* 184). The message underlying these editorial notes (and many others) could not be clearer: God demands teen girls' total and unquestioning obedience. Or else.

Along with being threatened if they disobey God, teen girl readers of *True Images* are also reminded that the threatened punishments will be good for them—God disciplines girls because he loves them, and girls should therefore be grateful. Couched in the language of love, this intimidating rhetoric of "obedience or else" serves to subordinate teen girls and sustain their dependence on God, all the while reinforcing the deity's authority and control. Thus a "Love Note" from God to teen girl readers referencing Deuteronomy 30:15–20 (God's blessings and curses for Israel) reads, "The choice is simple. Choose life or choose death. Choose to follow me or to go your own way. Live as though I don't exist and choose death. Love and obey me and choose life. It's up to you" (*TIB* 246). This life-or-death "love" note is less to do with "choice" than with threat, intimidation, and control.

The discourse of loving punishment also appears in the introductory notes to the book of Numbers, where readers are reminded that they must willingly accept the consequences of their disobedience:

> You may not always see the point of guidelines; at times, you might just want to blow them off entirely. That's when things get ugly. Disobedience brings discipline. But discipline is love in action—it helps you reevaluate your behaviour and learn from it … Real maturity and growth come from learning from your mistakes … and accepting discipline when it comes.
>
> (*TIB* 156)

Here, the threat of punishment is framed as "discipline"—a didactic lesson from which teen girls will learn and benefit. And discipline is equated with "love," thereby drawing an uncomfortable connection between punishment and affection. A similar message appears later in a "Dare to Believe" note, which reminds girls that God may punish them for their own good. "If you're never punished, your brat-potential could skyrocket," readers are warned. "Punished too much, and your confidence takes a nosedive. It's a good thing God gives just punishments. He's all about *balance*" (*TIB* 1049; emphasis original). Punishments are thus presented as both reasonable and necessary; girls should be willing recipients when God metes them out. Again, readers are rendered passive in the process; they are expected to be compliant and even grateful for God's total control and authority over them. Indeed, a "Genuine" note instructs girls that their obedience must be performed gladly and that they should be *grateful* for God's controlling influence in their lives: "God does have things he wants you to do or not do, but he wants you to obey him out of love and gratitude from your heart" (*TIB* 219). These messages invite girls to be complicit in their own coercive control, as well as reinforcing their dependency on God and their inability to leave this relationship.

While the *Revolve* Bible generally abstains from threatening its teen girl readers, the same language of "loving discipline" does appear from time to time. For example, Miriam's "Ladies of the Bible" profile (*RB* 168) tells us that God inflicted her with a terrible skin condition (Numbers 12) as a form of "discipline" after she dared to question Moses' (and thus God's) male authority. Girls are reminded that they ought to "respond to discipline" in a way that brings them "closer" to God—in other words, they should accept it. A "Daily Devos" note (titled "Father Knows Best," *RB* 210) reiterates this, letting readers know that "God's discipline is necessary for our growth," while the "Big Picture" overview of 1 Samuel warns that God "expects us to obey ... When we don't, we're brought to shame and failure" (*RB* 347). Similarly, in the 2 Kings "Big Picture" overview, girls are told that "some of us learn the hard way. We're warned about sin's consequences, but we don't listen. Only when the punishment comes do we realize that we should've obeyed God." But it's okay, girls are reassured, "discipline is just one of God's methods for shaping us into people who truly love and follow him!" (*RB* 459).

Despite this rhetoric of just and loving punishments, teen girl readers are left in no doubt that God is also to be feared. In *True Images*, they are advised to "'fear God and keep his commandments' [Ecclesiastes 12:13–14]. *That's* what you're here for. Fearing God means honoring and respecting and being in awe of him at all times" (*TIB* 873; emphasis original). Another "Dare to Believe" note reinforces this again: "God doesn't want you to be afraid of him. 'Fearing the Lord' means being aware of how utterly awesome he is. It means respecting his sovereignty and power" (*TIB* 809). Teen girls' fearful obedience is once again conflated with the honour, gratitude, and respect they must show for the deity's utter control over their lives.

Yet, given the various *True Images* threats we listed above, this reassurance that God doesn't want teen girls to be "afraid" of him reads as a ghastly form of gaslighting—another very common feature of coercive control—where perpetrators inundate their victims with conflicting messages, leaving them confused, disoriented, and doubting their own sanity.[4] Moreover, any possibility of a more equitable relationship with God—one based on some sense of mutual love and respect—is utterly rejected. Another "Dare to Believe" note alludes to Psalm 2:11 ("Serve the Lord with fear and celebrate his rule with trembling"), warning readers that "Some girls get so comfortable around God that they forget *who's in charge*. Yeah, he's a friend, but above all else, he's a holy God" (*TIB* 665; emphasis added). Again, the absolute and irrevocable power imbalance in this relationship is made absolutely clear, reminding teen girl readers that they ought to feel intimidated and subordinated in their every encounter with God.

"Don't trust your own talents and strength": humiliation and degradation as a means of control

Perpetrators of coercive control do not only rely on threats and intimidation to subordinate their victims. They also humiliate and degrade them too, by criticizing and shaming them (sometimes in front of others), magnifying and overstating their insecurities, treating them like a child, telling them that they are worthless, denying their ideas and opinions, and denigrating their strengths and achievements. A perpetrator may remind his victim that she is "nothing" without him, that no one else could love her as much as he does because she is so unlovable, and that her opinions are either stupid or wrong (Hayes and Jeffries 2015, 31–32; Stark 2007, 259–61). These degrading and humiliating messages are repeated over and over by the perpetrator, depleting his victim's sense of self-worth and making her believe that she is unworthy of respect, compassion, or a better relationship than the one she is currently in (Hayes and Jeffries 2015, 32; Hill 2019, ch. 1, iBook). This tactic is another means by which the perpetrator ensures his victim remains in the abusive relationship and becomes more dependent on him. It also allows him to reinforce his moral superiority and authority, by denying his victim any sense of self-respect and making her doubt her own strengths and abilities, particularly those of which she is proudest (Stark 2007, 258–59; Fontes 2015, 51).[5] Additionally, his victim's perceived ineptitude gives him justification for prioritizing his own needs over hers (Hayes and Jeffries 2015, 33).

These tactics of degradation and humiliation are visible on various occasions in *True Images*. Editorial inserts remind teen girls that they are bound to fail in life without God's help. This reinforces complementarian ideology, which warns girls and women not to upset or intimidate men by appearing smarter or more capable than them (Klein 2018, ch. 9, Kindle). This messaging also reinforces another objective of the evangelical purity movement (and purity culture more widely), which is to keep girls trapped in a patriarchal "perpetual girlhood" (Valenti 2009, 13). Girls are not encouraged to prepare themselves for autonomous adulthood but must remain eternally infantilized—controlled by their fathers, particularly their heavenly father, God. Indeed, in one of *Revolve*'s "Daily Devos," girls are reminded that God knows their "weaknesses and limitations ... So don't be in too big of a hurry to grow up—God may have a few things to teach you here and now" (*RB* 79). A few pages later, another "Daily Devos" note tells girls that God helps them fight their "battles," because "He already knows we can't do this life thing by ourselves, so don't try to be a heroine on your own!" (*RB* 87) While *Revolve* does occasionally promise readers that God wants them to achieve great things, they are also repeatedly told to "wait" for God to reveal his "plan" to them. As Stanley notes, rhetoric such as this serves to preserve "perpetual girlhood into adulthood, fostering a generational learned helplessness of feminine weakness, naivete, and ignorance" (2020, 121; see also Allen 2013).

True Images also likes to remind girls that they are prone to failure and don't have the capacity to help themselves. In a number of editorial notes, girls' abilities are downplayed, and their imagined ineptitude is magnified. In the introductory notes to the book of Joshua, for example, readers are told to "think of how many times *you really blow it* in life! *You drop the ball* with your family, friends and schoolwork *all the time*" (*TIB* 256; emphasis added). One "Genuine" note advises girls that if they are struggling to cope with all the pressures in their lives (school, family, conflicts of faith), they should "Take a lesson from the Israelites: Don't trust your own talents and strength; *those alone won't get you very far*. Instead, put your faith in God and trust him to lead you through life" (*TIB* 486; emphasis added). And in the "In Focus" profile (titled "C is for Clueless," *TIB* 274), we meet the fictional teen girl Danielle, who is unsure of what career she wants to pursue. Despite the normalcy of this uncertainty among teenagers, it is magnified and overstated here as a sign of teen girls' general ignorance and lack of knowledge about how to live their lives. The idea that girls could make choices for themselves is dismissed as unlikely—rather, they need to rely on their all-powerful male deity to take "control" of things for them. Readers are reassured that, "even when you feel totally clueless about what choices to make in life, God has it all under control."

True Images further reinforces girls' cluelessness about their futures in one of God's "Love Notes": "This time of your life can feel confusing—about what you want and feel, even about who you are. Focus on me. I understand you perfectly and will help you learn more about yourself. [Signed] The One who understands you" (*TIB* 805). Teen girls are reminded here that they are confused, unsure of what they want, what they should think, or who they are. They need to rely on God in order to "learn" about *themselves*, as though their self-identity is beyond their reach. Another "Dare to Believe" note likewise reinforces girls' dependence on the deity: "Ever had a problem you just couldn't solve? Forget the problem. Just focus on God, and then watch him take care of everything else in your life" (*TIB* 496). The *True Images*' God is a narcissistic God, who demands that teen girls "focus on" him and him alone. He also wants them to feel inadequate and helpless so that he can stay in control. "Feeling overwhelmed by responsibilities?" girls are asked. "Stay calm! Sometimes God intentionally throws us in the deep end so that we learn to rely on him to keep us afloat" (*TIB* 335). God clearly enjoys flinging girls into "the deep end," where they panic and flounder, just to remind them that they are utterly helpless and dependent on him.

Even when God occasionally praises girls, his praise is double-edged. For example, a "Love Note" linked to Genesis 1:27 reads, "My daughter, You are made in my image. You are worthy, not for what you own, not for your grades, not for your wardrobe ... but because I made you. [Signed] Your loving Father" (*TIB* 3). Girls' value is solely contingent on their ownership and creation by a male God—and in his image too—not because of anything they might achieve in their lives. They cannot even take any credit for their own academic or sartorial successes. God's "I made you" comment here is both a claim of ownership and a call for gratitude. It also reminds girls that they are utterly dependent on God, not only for their successes and achievements but for their very life itself. And the father-daughter language used in this "Love Note" (and many others too) reinforces male headship and authority in the family realm, hinting that girls are likewise owned by and dependent on their *earthly* father. The love note is followed by a question for girls to ponder: "How does this truth change how you view yourself?" Framed as a "truth," this message to teen girls about their dependence and lack of self-achievement becomes non-negotiable, and readers are asked to revision their own sense of self through this deeply troubling lens.

If girls have not gotten the message already that they are nothing without God, don't worry! *True Images* keeps reminding teen girls that any personal triumphs they do achieve are never down to their own abilities but should always be credited to God. In one "Dare to Believe" note, girls are told, "God doesn't want you, or your team, or your family, or your church to take the credit. He wants the credit. He wants the glory. So let him have it! You'll be amazed what he can do with it" (*TIB* 296). God is portrayed here as an unpleasant man-child tyrant, who refuses to let *anyone* feel good about their own achievements. The fact that teen girls are told here to "let him have" the credit reinforces complementarian concerns that girls' successes may undermine male superiority and authority. Another "Dare to Believe" note makes a similar statement: "Sometimes when you've worked hard for something, it's tempting to gloat over your success. Instead, remember where your success really comes from" (*TIB* 508). This is reiterated yet again in an "In Focus" profile featuring a girl called Natasha who wants to do well in life, keep her grades up, study hard, and get into a great college. But that's not good enough, we are told, because she is basing her life on earthly successes rather than her faith in Jesus. Everything else in a girl's life, her "talents, achievements, looks, family and possessions—is temporary" (*TIB* 570). Girls are reminded that God only accepts you "because of his grace—not because of anything you do." Moreover, "Jesus isn't looking for girls who think they've got it all together; he longs for girls who know they need him." Jesus prefers needy girls, it seems, not girls who are smart, competent, autonomous, and ambitious.

This undermining of girls' self-worth or capabilities comes out again in another "Genuine" note, where girls are told that "God wants you to remember that all your talents come from him … *every* good thing that you have or do is a gift from God (see James 1:17)—and remember to thank him!" (*TIB* 221; emphasis original). These gifts include material possessions, as well as talents (making friends, musical ability, being a straight-A student). Girls are not allowed to forget that these aren't personal achievements but are *given* to them by God. They are *nothing* without him. This is again reinforced in a "Love Note," where God tells girls they are his "treasured possession. Out of the whole earth, which is mine, I chose you—not because of anything you've done, but out of my mercy and love. Love, Dad" (93). The reader is both a "loved one" and a "possession" of her Dad-God—a God who likes to remind her of his own omnipotence (the "whole earth" belongs to him) and *her* respective powerlessness. God loves her *despite* the fact that she has not done anything special—in fact, his love is based on his "mercy," as though she were already a lost cause. This implies that she should be grateful that her Dad-God loves her at all, because, no one else is likely to. Just as a perpetrator of coercive control denigrates his victim's successes and reminds her that she is "nothing" without him, the *True Images* God sends the exact same message to his teen girl readers.

True Images also indulges in a high level of gaslighting around this issue of teen girls' self-confidence. In a "Genuine" note on "Confidence" (which seems to be a bad thing for a girl to have), girls are warned not to be too self-confident: "If God calls you to do something for him, then he must think you're right for the job—even if you doubt yourself. He doesn't want your confidence to be based on your abilities or looks or status. He wants you to be confident in him" (*TIB* 333), In other words, he wants you to be dependent. And in one of this Bible's glossy inserts (tucked between pp. 430 and 431), girls are made privy to "God's Thoughts on Confidence." These read: "You can do all things through my Son, who gives you strength"; "I've given you power, love and self-discipline through my Spirit"; and "You can come to me confidently, just ask." None of these actually speak to the reader's *own* abilities or sense of self-confidence—anything they can do, any "power, love and self-discipline" they have, comes from God, not from within. The confidence being promoted here to teen girls is not self-confidence at all—it is a dependent confidence in God. This is also reinforced by the note of advice written just above these quotes: "Base your self-confidence on God, not on yourself. You'll do lots of dumb and embarrassing things in life (and that's okay!), but God never will." And again, in a "Genuine" note on "Confidence," girls are asked if they are self-confident or "*God*-confident":

> Most people see being "self-confident" as a good thing. But that's really not how God wants you to see yourself. Now, don't misunderstand. God doesn't want you to be insecure and unsure. But he does want you to find your confidence in *him* and in what *he* can do in and through you. There's a big difference between having confidence in yourself and having confidence in God … When you rely on yourself, you'll only go so far. But when you rely on God, there's no limit to how far you can go!
>
> (*TIB* 54; emphasis original)

The mixed messages and gaslighting here are exhausting to navigate. Girls ought not have confidence in themselves, but God doesn't want them to be insecure either. Girls are reminded that they cannot rely on themselves ("you'll only go so far") because they are inadequate. Through denigrating girls' abilities, this editorial note drives home the complementarian belief in female subordination as a divinely ordained imperative, and essentially tells teen girls that they must rely on a male authority figure to make anything of their lives, or feel good about themselves, because they are simply not good enough on their own. If teen girls have any confidence left after this barrage of confounding instructions, God demands all the credit.

Further gaslighting occurs on numerous occasions throughout *True Images*, as girls are told they are special in God's eyes, but not that special; they are ordinary but extraordinary, perfect but flawed, loved by God, despite their inherent "ugliness." It is praise and denigration at the same time, echoing the coercive controller's insistence to his victim that she is unlovable and should feel grateful that at least *he* loves her. In one "Love Note," God tells readers, "My love and mercy are infinite. My love extends to all who come to me—the disabled, the weak, the fatherless, the unlovely, the strangers, the sinners. (You fall into at least that last category, dear.) Always know that I love you" (*TIB* 224). The ableist language here is perturbing, casting "the disabled" among the "sinners," the "weak," and the "unlovely." Additionally, the parenthetical statement reminds teen girls that they are essentially unworthy of love—a "sinner" at the very least—so should be grateful for God's love. This is also articulated in a *Revolve* "Daily Devos" note, which tells readers that "God saw you, in all your sinful ugliness, and loved you anyway (before you were beautiful)! His love, grace, and mercy transformed you ... suddenly you were no longer ugly and unlovable. Because of Christ, you're pure and lovely, a treasure in God's eyes" (*RB* 1501; emphasis original). Without God in their lives, girls are "ugly and unlovable," utterly dependent on the deity for their own sense of self-worth. A *True Images* "Dare to Believe" note likewise makes this clear: "It's pointless to keep secrets from God. He already knows all the ugly details of your life ... and he still loves you! Go ahead—show him the real you" (*TIB* 325). Girls' lives are again identified as being "ugly," but readers are reassured that God is willing to love them, regardless. The reminder that it is "pointless" trying to hide anything from God is also coercive language, portraying the deity as a stalker-surveiller from whom girls simply cannot escape (more on this later).

There is another way that *True Images* and *Revolve* degrade and humiliate its teen girl readers. Just as coercive controllers constantly denigrate their victims' opinions, ideas, and words, some editorial inserts in these Bibles tell girls to stop talking, because they are prone to saying the wrong thing. Again, this may tap into complementarian anxieties about teen girls sounding as though they are smarter than teen guys or using their voices to claim some personal autonomy. *True Images* knocks this on the head by teaching girls to guard their tongues, as though their very act of speaking was an affront against the Lord. One "Dare to Believe" note warns readers that "You can avoid a lot of hurt feelings and regrets if you just keep that mouth shut!" (*TIB* 800). Another note cites Psalm 39:1 (where the psalmist says they will put a "muzzle" on their mouth in the presence of the wicked), telling readers: "Not sure a muzzle would be a smart fashion choice. You might want to try controlling your tongue without one: no gossip, no hurtful words, no backtalk. You can do it!" (*TIB* 701). The mention of "muzzling" girls' mouths is deeply discomforting, despite the encouraging phrase at the end with its jaunty exclamation point. This hostile rhetoric is repeated in another "Genuine" note, which states that "You can tell a lot about a girl by listening to what she says and how she says it … Every time you get ready to *open that mouth of yours*, think about what you're going to say and what that says about you" (*TIB* 830; emphasis added). Meanwhile, a *Revolve* "Daily Devos" note (titled "Put a Lid on It, Smarty," *RB* 739) tells girls that "too much chatter is sure to lead to sin because our mouths are a hotbed of trouble. When we don't control our words, they will eventually lead to catastrophe." Catastrophe? Really? Another "Daily Devos" note ("Blabbermouth," *RB* 903) tells girls that "if you have a tendency to talk and talk and not say much, then you might want to examine that part of your life." It offers girls the following advice: "Don't interrupt! Wait for someone to finish his or her thought before you pipe in," and "Think carefully before you speak," as though girls are bound to say stupid things. Both these Bibles repeatedly attempt to silence teen girls' voices, making them doubt the veracity and appropriateness of their words, and warning them to think long and hard before they even consider opening their mouths.

These are just some examples of the editorial inserts in *Revolve* and *True Images* that (unintentionally perhaps) serve to degrade and humiliate girls. I don't have room here to list them all but will leave you with a final example from *True Images*. A "Dare to Believe" note reminds readers that "God loves it when a girl recognizes her smallness next to him and at the same time offers him her *best* in everything she does" (*TIB* 524; emphasis original). The *True Images* God loves girls to know how insignificant they are, because it keeps them in their subordinate place and makes them more dependent on him. With all their flaws, who else could possibly love them?

"Locking eyes with the Lord": love-bombing

While coercive controllers inundate their victims with threats, denigration, and intimidation, they also ensure victims' loyalty by manipulating them with flourishes of love language and reassurances of devotion. This behaviour is never carried out with the intent of nurturing mutual love and commitment; rather, as Hayes and Jeffries note, it is a malignant grooming tactic similar to those adopted by paedophiles, which involves perpetrators making repeated and exaggerated displays of "intense starry-eyed interest" in order to "lure the victims into their trap" (2015, 38; citing Hennessy 2012, 77). A controller may bombard his victim with flattery, gifts, romantic language and gestures, declarations of love, and desire for total commitment. By grooming his victim thus, he ensures her devotion and loyalty, all the while bringing her under his control. When the threats, degradation, and other abuses eventually begin, the victim is left confused and disorientated; her controller may blame her for the abuse, so she tries even harder to please and placate him in the hope that his "loving" behaviour will recommence (Hayes and Jeffries 2015, 39; Hill 2019, ch. 1, iBook). A perpetrator may alternate abuse and love-bombing, creating a "mercurial" cycle of rewards and punishments, further confusing and gaslighting his victim until she feels she is constantly "walking on eggshells," scared of what to expect next (Hill 2019, ch. 1, iBook; Hayes and Jeffries 2015, 39). Any act of kindness or declaration of love will be interpreted by her as a "sign" that things are getting better and the relationship is worth holding onto; she therefore tries even harder to please her controller and conform to his demands in the hope that he will repeat his loving behaviours and never punish her again (Hill, ch. 1, iBook). The victim may even begin to feel grateful whenever her controller shows her some comfort or kindness, paradoxically viewing him as her "saviour," simply because he has stopped abusing her for now (Hill 2019, ch. 1, iBook).

Hayes and Jeffries (2015) describe coercive control as a form of "romantic terrorism"; perpetrators use love-bombing as an important tactic to keep their victims terrorized and controlled. In the *True Images* and *Revolve* Bibles, readers are likewise romantically terrorized by a mercurial God, who interweaves his threats and criticisms with profuse declarations of love. Moreover, this "love talk" often takes on a strangely romantic tone. While sexual purity is prioritized in these Bibles, romance with God is perfectly fine, even desirable, for teen girls to embrace.

The romantic language used in *Revolve* and *True Images* encourages teen girl readers to envision God as a "perfect" romantic partner, framing the reader's relationship with the deity as deeply intimate, even sexualized. But it is a relationship based on a power imbalance, with girls cast as the needy, dependent partner and God as the source of their salvation. In a *True Images* "Genuine" note, girls are reminded that if life is stressing them out, "focus on God's faithfulness and power to overcome any problem. And after locking eyes with the Lord, you'll find that you can face the world again—unafraid" (*TIB* 687). On the same page, a "Dare to Believe" note asks girl readers, "Do you need some Face-Time with God? You don't have to wait for his call. He's already said, 'come and talk with me. Let's get to know each other'" (*TIB* 687). This is not terribly subtle. If someone invited me to "lock eyes" with them so we could "get to know each other," I'd be unlikely to interpret their invitation as a chaste request for friendship.

Some of the love-bombing expressed in *True Images* is far less subtle than this, though. God, girls are told, "wants you to love him with all that you are. He wants to have an intimate relationship with you. Your love relationship with God is real worship" (*TIB* 932). It's fascinating that romantic "love" is equated with "worship" here, as it implies this is part of an ideal romantic relationship. It's not a mutual "worship," though—there is only room for one object of devotion in a divine-teen girl relationship. There is no space for girls' consent either; God *wants* an "intimate relationship" with a teenage girl; what she wants is not mentioned, and how is she expected to withhold her consent from the *deity*?

Similar "romantic" overtones are expressed repeatedly in *Revolve*. God's love is described as "more passionate than we can imagine" (*RB* 786). Whether girls realize it or not, God has been "romancing" them their entire life: "Day and night he pursues you, demonstrating his love for you" (*RB* 1338). Pursuit smacks of stalking, but here it is normalized, even sacralized. Readers are told that "It thrills [God] to spend time with you. He runs to see you and loves to tell others that *you are his*" (*RB* 1135; emphasis added). Again, the deity's love is framed in terms of ownership and control. It is also terrifyingly obsessive and extreme; one "Daily Devos" note (*RB* 1135) tells readers that God "sacrificed his only Son" just so he can "be together for eternity" with his favourite teen girls. This is repeated in another "Daily Devos" note (titled "Prince Charming Has Arrived") which again reminds readers that God "sent Jesus to die so you could live happily ever after with him" (*RB* 1138). God's love is so powerfully obsessive he is prepared to utilize violence to achieve its ends; there is something threatening and utterly terrifying in the intensity of these claims. They also reverberate disturbingly with another "Daily Devos" note that tells readers God wants them to be "so in love with him that they're willing to give him *their* lives" (*RB* 653; emphasis added).

When girls' *earthly* dates and boyfriends are brought up, it is clear that *Revolve* and *True Images* are less than impressed. Because God is meant to take first place in a girl's life, not some random teenage guy. In the *True Images* introductory notes to Song of Songs, girls are given the following message: "As you read this love story, pray that if God has a guy in your future, that he will love you with passion and romance—and set your heart on the God who already does" (*TIB* 874). Lest we forget, the *True Images* God is a jealous God, who does not want teen girls' attention to stray too far from him. This is also echoed in *Revolve*; one "Daily Devos" note (*RB* 785) describes Song of Songs as a "pretty steamy love poem" that reminds girls to not let their "emotions run wild" before they are ready for marriage (because that would "just lead to trouble"). And while girls might have a crush on a guy, they are cautioned to "make sure that you don't forget that God should be your first love! Instead of going nuts over guys, focus on your relationship with [God]. He'll satisfy your desire to be deeply known and loved" until he decides to let you (eventually, maybe) meet the "right man."

If girls don't get the message here that God wants to be their first and only love, *True Images* and *Revolve* offers several further reminders to keep them in check. One of *Revolve*'s "Daily Devos" notes (titled "Cheating on God?" *RB* 681) sends girls a stern warning:

> We can't even conceive how worthy God is of our devotion. Yet we keep flirting with our old boyfriend ... with the world. God's got every right to be intolerant of unfaithfulness. He'll be jealous of our affection until we give him our full devotion ... it's what God deserves. Don't mess around with the world and act like you belong to it. Only God is worthy of all your devotion!

Similar sentiments are expressed in a *True Images* glossy insert (between pp. 174 and 175), where we find a quiz to help girls work out what their ideal "Prince Charming" might look like. This is followed by a "Love Advice Column," ostensibly written by some older "big sisters" (women in their late teens, 20s and 30s). The advice given includes, "Be open to who God has in mind for you" (i.e. God gets to choose whom you date), and "You don't need a guy to complete you!

God completes you—only him." Girls are warned that there is no such thing as a "perfect guy," so they should "Focus on your identity as God's girl—and let God bring someone along for you *if* and when the timing's right" (emphasis added).[6] Even in that most intimate sphere of personal and romantic relationships, God is there, calling the shots, making sure that no one takes his place as the object of a teen girl's devotion. These demands for relationship exclusivity also serve to isolate girls from their peers—a common tactic of coercive controllers, which I discuss further in the next section.

The God presented to us in *True Images* and *Revolve* is a God of power and control, a jealous God who wants teen girls to recognize his omnipotence; but he also showers them with promises of love and desire. The ideal romantic relationship, it seems, involves a massive power imbalance between an omnipotent male figure and an utterly powerless girl. This leaves no room for consent nor does it give teen girls any agency to navigate their *own* sexual selves or choose their *own* romantic relationships. It's God or no one.

"You belong to me, and I will never leave you": isolation and microregulation

Perpetrators of coercive control use various methods to isolate their victims from family, friends, and significant others, until victims' personal support networks are reduced to one: their controller. As Fontes notes, "A controlling man feels threatened when his partner's life does not revolve entirely around his own. He tries to control her movements, achievements, and connections with others" (2015, 14). A controller may isolate his victim by setting up tests of loyalty, interpreting her requests to spend time with other people as a sign of her infidelity (Fontes 2015, 17, 20). She may therefore begin policing her own behaviour—avoiding social contact, changing the way she dresses, or turning down invitations from family and friends, all to avoid having to deal with the repercussions of her controller's extreme jealousy (Fontes 2015, 20; Hayes and Jeffries 2015, 35).

Isolation is hugely effective in ensuring that a victim of coercive control will have very little opportunity to disclose her abuse and thus get the help and support she needs. It may also reinforce her sense of dependence on her controller, who will remind her that she is now exclusively "his" (Stark 2007, 262; Hayes and Jeffries 2015, 34). When he cuts off her access to other resources and support, he also compels her to make *him* and *his* needs central to her life, while her own personal interests and friendships are discouraged or interrupted (Fontes 2015, 15;

Hayes and Jeffries 2015, 36). As Jess Hill notes, "As long as the victim maintains meaningful social and emotional connections, the abuser's influence is diluted. To become the most powerful person in her life, he must eliminate her external sources of support and silence voices that would question his behaviour" (2019, ch. 1, iBook). Through isolating his victim, the perpetrator effectively ensures that he becomes the only means by which she can make sense of what is happening to her, or even make sense of herself. Isolation also limits the ways victims can express themselves or seek affirmation about the abusiveness of their relationship. Thus, according to Stark, "The victim of coercive control is isolated from the moorings of her identity and, because identity is first and foremost a social construction, from her own unique personhood" (2007, 262).

A perpetrator isolates his victim to keep her away from others, but also to keep her more closely in his sights, thereby restricting her freedom and autonomy (Fontes 2015, 16; Hayes and Jeffries 2015, 33). An isolated victim finds it increasingly difficult to locate places, spaces, and times to be alone, as her controller insists that he must always be with her, involving himself in the activities she may otherwise do herself, such as going to class or work, meeting friends, shopping, and even having a bath (Fontes 2015, 16). He might insert himself into those everyday activities traditionally associated with women's and girls' lives, including what they choose to wear, their appearance,and the friendships and relationships they value (Stark 2007, 5; Hayes and Jeffries 2015, 37). A woman's controller thus invades *all* her personal spaces, taking away anything (a place, a time, even a piece of clothing) that gives her a sense of freedom or meaning in her life. Instead, she is compelled to put him first, over and above her own needs (Hayes and Jeffries 2015, 33). Such microregulation can destroy the victim's sense of autonomy and agency, leaving "little space for personhood to breathe" (Stark, 2007, 274).

Isolation and microregulation are horribly effective ways of undermining the victim's relational self, her social agency, and her subjectivity. At their heart, they render her "unable to choose how and where she will relate to other people" (Fontes 2015, 16). The perpetrator may isolate and regulate his victim incrementally, so that she does not even realize it is happening in the first place. Or she may simply see it as evidence of her controller's love and devotion. As Hayes and Jeffries note, "Keeping your partner close every minute of the day because being away from them is too much to bear, expressions of jealousy, demanding the prioritization of the relationship, excluding pre-existing friendships so that every waking moment can be spent together—all of this can be interpreted as an endearing demonstration of love" (2015, 35; also Fontes 2015, 35; Stark 2007, 267). Particularly when a victim is young, vulnerable, or relatively powerless, a controller can justify these isolation tactics as a means of keeping her safe (Fontes 2015, 15). But in such a relationship, she is anything but safe.

The editorial inserts throughout *True Images* and *Revolve* reinforce this need for girls to be isolated from the world. Contemporary secular culture in all its forms (including fashion, movies, celebrity culture, and non-Christian friends) are consistently denigrated as vacuous distractions, sources of threat and temptation, or the trappings of a sinful life. And despite all the threats that are made to girls if they fail to please God (discussed earlier), they are also reminded that the deity is their only source of safety. In one *True Images* "Love Note," God reminds readers, "At times, the world doesn't seem like a safe place to live. At times, it feels like more people are against you than for you. Don't lose hope. I'll plant you in a safe place" (*TIB* 373). This is reiterated in another "Love Note," as girls are warned against seeking various forms of "fake satisfaction," including "drugs and alcohol, relationships, shopping, money, entertainment" (*TIB* 768). "But if you want true satisfaction," God continues, "choose me. I'll provide you with lasting good things." It is interesting here that "relationships" are equated with the more negative "drugs and alcohol," as though all these things are equally unsatisfactory. God's promise of "lasting good things" and his offer to give girls "true satisfaction" smack of creepy love talk and reinforce the deity's demand for relationship exclusivity. These *True Images* notes echo the rhetoric used in relationships of coercive control to convince victims that the world is a dangerous place and that they will only be safe with their controller.

The *True Images* God likewise does not want teen girls to listen to others, especially if it means they stop listening to *him*, even for a second. Here are just a few more examples from various editorial notes in *True Images* (I don't have space to include them all, but believe me, there are many others):

> I love it when you choose my opinion over the opinion of others! [Signed] The One whose opinion counts.
>
> (*TIB* 346)

> If you're asking people's advice 24/7 but never going straight to God, you're bound to fail. Since all wisdom comes from God, why not go straight to the source?
>
> (*TIB* 642)

Expecting anything (or *anyone*) other than God to give you joy and contentment will always lead to disappointment.

(*TIB* 680; emphasis original)

Looking for the perfect friend? You may be setting yourself up for disappointment. Even your most faithful amiga can let you down sometimes. Only God is 100 percent perfectly trustworthy.

(*TIB* 779)

Instead of searching futilely for that one flawless guy, friend or parent, try trusting in a perfect God. Your chances of finding him are much better!

(*TIB* 891)

Similar messages crop up repeatedly in *Revolve* too, where girls keep being reminded that God is the only one they can rely on, rather than anyone else, because "He's the one who can save and help you" (*RB* 655). Their earthly support networks are continually undermined—a common isolating tactic used by coercive controllers. In one "Daily Devos" note, readers are reminded that "every person you ever count on is going to let you down ... because they're just human" (*RB* 345). People will "mess up eventually," no matter how hard they try to make you happy, but girls are reassured that God will "*never* let you down" (emphasis original). Even parents and families are not immune to God's critique: they "let their kids down" (*RB* 210), they "don't act like they love each other" (*RB* 718), and they can "have big problems" (*RB* 756). God, on the other hand, is the "ultimate parent ... perfect at this parenting gig" (*RB* 210; also 931); he is "the best father ever—and you belong to him" (*RB* 1153); and he will "pick up the slack left by your earthly parents" (*RB* 856).

So, while teen girl readers of *Revolve* and *True Images* are encouraged to respect their parents, make friends with other Christian girls, or speak to trusted adults if they are in trouble, they are also gaslighted into believing that these family members, friends, and support networks *cannot* and *ought not* take the place of God in their lives. In a relationship of coercive control, this tactic also serves to reiterate the intense jealousy of the controller, which itself may be a source of fear or intimidation for the victim.

And make no mistake, the God of *True Images* and *Revolve* is a jealous God. He wants teen girls all to himself. He wants their attention and their time—*all* the time. *Revolve* readers are warned to let go of things that give them pleasure, such as a particular activity or friendship, because "if it's taking God's spot of top priority in your life, it's an idol" (*RB* 881). Instead, they should walk with God, "turn to him first in everything ... And he'll show you how to fill the holes in your heart with him." This is repeated in another "Daily Devos" note, which reminds girls that things like make-up, clothes, friendships, and hobbies are false idols that threaten girls' loyalty to God: "God wants your heart to be all his, and he's not going to share you with anything or anyone else. So take a look at your priorities and give God the place he deserves: *numero uno!*" (*RB* 950; emphasis original). Girls have to live under God's authority in everything; they are instructed to "make God the boss of your life ... He cares about your future and wants you to consult him and follow what he tells you to do" (*RB* 325). Elsewhere in *Revolve*, readers are told to "Listen to the one true God's commands for your life and keep all your devotion and adoration focused on him. He alone deserves your worship!" (*RB* 273). They are also advised to be ready for "total surrender" to God, who "requires full commitment" (*RB* 455). Most disturbingly, they are encouraged to stand apart from their friendships and devote themselves totally to God: "It might be a little lonely at times, but God will be your best friend" (*RB* 777). In other words, God wants to isolate you from everyone you know so he can have you all to himself.

Similar messages are repeated in *True Images*. One "Genuine" note reminds girls that they must put God at the centre of their lives, policing their words to ensure that they don't spend too much time talking about "clothes, fashion and friends" or their favourite TV show, music, or celebrity rather than talking about God: "As you go through your day chatting away, what part does God play in your conversations?" (*TIB* 503). Girls are expected to think and talk about God more than anything else—or else. They must never forget that they owe God everything and can only find happiness through him: "[God] wants you to find your joy *in him*. You see, all the good things that you experience come *from his hand*, and he intends for you to enjoy them as gifts *from him*. He wants you to celebrate the life that *he has given you* and to find your satisfaction *in him*" (*TIB* 861; emphasis added). In these two short sentences, girls are reminded five times that God is the only source of their happiness. The God of *True Images* persistently demands teen girls' undivided and exclusive attention. He never wants to be treated as "second best," only getting girls' "leftover time" (*TIB* 231); he does not want to "share" girls with their "other loves and desires," but insists that their lives be "offered to him fully" (*TIB* 1163); he "doesn't like the back burner," but needs to be at the "top of the list" (*TIB* 1271); he "wants first priority in [their] life. He's never content with second place" (*TIB* 1271).

Girls' isolation is fostered further when they are encouraged to spend all their alone-time with God. In the *True Images* "Dare to Believe" note related to Genesis 2:3 (God's creation of the Sabbath), readers are told that "taking a break" is a divine command. But the "break" must be spent with God: "Unplug entirely—a device-free hour, just you and God" (*TIB* 3). This is repeated again in a "Love Note" that refers to Exodus 31:12 (the law to observe the Sabbath): "This week, make the Sabbath a time to relax, remember and reconnect with me. It's our special day. Love, Dad" (*TIB* 108). Even when girls are resting, they cannot escape their ever-present Dad-God. Again, control is couched in the language of love to soften its coercive core.

This discourse of coercive isolation is repeated in another "Love Note" that is one of the most disturbing editorial contributions to *True Images*: "My girl, Shut off your device. Close the laptop. Turn off your phone and close your bedroom door. Now come to me and be quiet. Do you hear me? [Signed] Father God" (*TIB* 709). This series of six commands in rapid succession seem designed to intimidate girls, control their actions, sequester them, silence them, and trap them in a space with their controller. "Father God" is isolating his "girl" and inserting himself into one of her most private spaces—her bedroom. Without her phone or laptop, she has no means of reaching out to anyone else for help. She has to "come to" God and "be quiet"—she cannot refuse, call for help, or withhold her consent. The bedroom setting evokes disturbing images of sexual abuse, while the final "Do you hear me?" is deeply intimidating. Were anyone else to send a teenage girl a "love note" like this, we would contact the police. Immediately. Yet here in *True Images*, the language of grooming and coercive control is normalized and sanctified.

These last four paragraphs also offer some perfect illustrations of microregulation; the evangelical God constructed by these Bibles inveigles his way into every single aspect of a teen girl's life, depriving her of privacy, regulating her activities, cutting her off from family and friends, and never leaving her alone. She has no ability to withhold her consent to this intrusion but must bend to the will of her Father-God. She cannot make choices of her own but must "ask" God to make decisions for her and accept that what he chooses to give her may not be what she wants. In one *True Images* "Love Note," God tells readers, "My child ... I may not give you everything you want, but I will give you what you need and what is best for you" (*TIB* 523). The "My child" address infantilizes teen girls, justifying God's control over their lives. And should girls query God's decisions, they are warned that the consequences may not be pleasant. Another "Dare to Believe" note makes this clear: "If God says no to a relationship, a job or anything, you know it's the best answer for you. Rebelling against God's decision will only hurt you in the end" (*TIB* 624). The warning is repeated in a "Genuine" note on obedience, which again attempts to microregulate teen girls' lives, advising them that their bad behaviours (white lies, cheating on a paper, sending "sexy" photos of themselves) "have a way of coming back to haunt you" (*TIB* 272). They are reminded that "even if your sin doesn't seem like a big deal now, it is. If God says to get rid of it, do it" (*TIB* 272).

The God in *Revolve* also microregulates girls' actions by telling them they must do what he commands, because he is "in control." In a *Revolve* "Daily Devos" note (ironically titled "Control Freak," referring to girls themselves), girls are warned that "if you're still fighting with God for control of your life, it's time to let go and let him take the steering wheel" because they are a "child of God, [they] are his. He is in control" (*RB* 896). The same note ends with the direction "Make a conscious decision to choose God above everything else." This "God is in control" refrain is relentless in *Revolve*, and while it is often framed in the rhetoric of compassion and care, it is also exhausting and demoralizing. One "Daily Devos" note even warns that girls who refuse to let God microregulate their lives may well find themselves in trouble. Readers are informed that, after they accept Jesus into their lives, God equips them with a spiritual GPS (Global Positioning System); the Holy Spirit, "comes to live inside of you. He gives you directions every day—people he wants you to talk to, places you should or shouldn't go, and he even tells you which things you should and shouldn't do" (*RB* 830). And while this note tells girls that they can "choose" whether or not to follow the directions on this GPS, they are warned that if they fail to do so, they will get "lost in the dark woods of sin and rebellion."

True Images is also relentless in its messages to girls about God's control. In one "Love Note," God tells his "Chosen one" that "I have chosen you for a specific purpose. It may not be clear to you yet, but trust me. I am in control" (*TIB* 602). And in the Virgin Mary's "Mirror Images" profile, girls are advised to say the following prayer: "Dear Jesus, sometimes I'm afraid of letting you have complete control of my life. Show me how to be a girl who always says yes to you. Amen" (*TIB* 903). Teen girls are being instructed to relinquish control of their lives and their agency, so that God can microregulate everything they do. The "just say yes" language used here is also disturbing, given its allusions to sexual coercion and girls' lack of consent (particularly in light of its association here with the Virgin Mary traditions, which testify to her non-consensual impregnation).

God's control and microregulation of teen girls' lives sometimes extends inside their bodies too. As well as its description of the spiritual GPS that God puts within them, a "Daily Devos" note reiterates that God lives in girls' hearts, so girls must make sure they are good enough for him:

> Ask yourself if the current state of God's home inside you is a place he would feel comfortable. Do any of your current habits limit his free reign in your life? Are there any areas of sin you try to keep hidden under lock and key, hoping he won't venture into these rooms? If you truly want God to feel at home inside you, commit to obey him in everything.
>
> (*RB* 1022)

This invasive imagery is likewise echoed in a *True Images* "Dare to Believe" note. Likening girls' hearts to playdough, readers are told to "Make sure your heart is soft and pliable for God, so he can do magnificent things with you" (79). The tactile imagery of girls' hearts as a "soft and pliable" plaything for God to manipulate and do "things with" is really quite discomforting, as is the idea that internal bodily spaces are not beyond God's invasion and control. Playdough conjures notions of something passive, yielding, touchable, squeezable, not to mention frivolous and disposable. This sculpting metaphor is repeated in a "Genuine" note portraying God as a controlling "potter" who moulds and shapes girls' lives and bodies, regardless of their own desires:

> In making a piece of pottery, does the clay fight back? Of course not! The potter is always in charge. In life, God is in charge. Always. God is God, and *you* are not. He has the right to decide how things go in your life because he's the Potter, and you are the clay ... The clay's job is to trust and submit to the Potter. God knows what he's doing as he's shaping you. Trust him with the outcome.
>
> (*TIB* 960; emphasis original)

Here, girls' agency over their lives is utterly denied. God is "in charge. Always" and he has "the right" to control them; girls' only option is to "submit." The embodied nature of the deity's control is repeated in a "Love Note" warning girls not to "abuse" their bodies with drugs, alcohol, eating disorders, or "anything sexually immoral" (thereby disturbingly equating eating disorders with immorality). Girls are then reminded that "You belong to me, and I live within you. Care for your body in a way that honors me" (*TIB* 1522). There is no escape from this invasive deity, who is everywhere, including *inside* girls' bodies. Like coercive controllers who colonize their victims' private spaces, God takes it a step further and colonizes and invades girls at the most personal and embodied level. He even manages to get *inside* them. Their bodies are no longer their own.

"You're completely transparent": microsurveillance

In coercively controlling relationships, the perpetrator will subject his victim to a high level of scrutiny and surveillance, constantly checking where she is, what she is doing, who she is spending time with, even what she is thinking and feeling. This tactic (closely interwoven with microregulation) is used to deprive the victim of any sense of privacy or personal autonomy and allows the perpetrator to dominate his victim's life entirely (Fontes 2015, 27). He may call his victim repeatedly throughout the day (or insist that she call him at set times), question her in granular detail about her daily movements, thoughts, and interactions, or track her activity on social media. Even her most private spaces (diaries, phones, computers, closets, and drawers) are surveilled, regulated, and invaded. A perpetrator may even download a tracking app onto his victim's mobile device (without her knowledge) so that he can "watch" her from afar, and intimidate and terrorize her with his seemingly "god-like power" and extraordinary knowledge about her every move (Hill 2019, ch. 1, iBook; also Fontes 2015, 30).

This microsurveillance, as Stark (2007) calls it, serves to convince the victim that her controller is omnipotent, omniscient, and omnipresent, thereby enforcing her behavioural compliance to his demands and reminding her that she can never escape his gaze *or* his grasp, even when they are not physically together (Hill 2019, ch. 1, iBook). All her personal spaces (her work, her school, her favourite coffee shops—anywhere she goes to get away from her controller) are gradually colonized through his microsurveillance, with the effect that he gains the power to increasingly shape and control her world and reality. For the microsurveiller, intimate relationships are seen as "a zero-sum game in which each sign of a partner's separateness is interpreted as something taken from [him]" (Stark 2007, 257). A perpetrator may use microsurveillance to discover any hint of his victim's disobedience or disloyalty, invading her everyday routines in a way that "obliterate" her autonomy and agency (Stark 2007, 257). As Stark notes, "If abusive relationships were filmed in slow motion, they would resemble a grotesque dance whereby victims create moments of autonomy and perpetrators 'search and destroy' them" (217).

While the tactic of microsurveillance is less apparent (or at least less explicitly expressed) in *Revolve*, teen girl readers of the *True Images* Bible will be left in no doubt that God is watching them—*always*.[7] And God's gaze is not always benign or loving, not least because it is omnipresent and inescapable. It's as though he has downloaded that tracking app (mentioned previously) onto every girl's life. Indeed, one particular "Love Note" seems to admit as much. "Beloved," writes God, "There are no secrets between us—absolutely none. I can see every text you send, every picture you post, and every thought you think" (*TIB* 518). Even girls' private thoughts are not beyond God's scrutiny. Beneath this note, girls are told to "talk honestly with God about any secret you might have. It's okay—he already knows." If our suspicions weren't aroused enough already, *True Images* make it even more explicit in the following "Genuine" note, which asks girls to think about their commitment to God: "We can say we're committed and even convince ourselves that we are, but when it comes down to it, God knows. His ultimate surveillance system [referencing 2 Chronicles 16:9] searches the entire earth" (*TIB* 538). Girls are reminded here that that they need to commit to God "100 percent, 24/7," nothing else will do—and God will *always* know if they fail in this duty, because they are *always* under his omniscient and ever-present gaze.

The 100 "Love Notes" scattered throughout *True Images* also regularly reinforce God's surveilling eye. Here are some examples:

> My child, You may not see me at work in your circumstances. You may not be aware that I am there. But I am.
> (*TIB* 447)

> My daughter, I never sleep. I never take a vacation or go on a break or ask for a substitute. I watch over you constantly. I see you come and go—I'm always caring, loving, protecting you 24/7.
> (*TIB* 788)

> My girl, Ever wish that life was straight-up easier? I know your paths—where you've been, where you are, where you're going—and I'm making you into something beautiful throughout it all.
> (*TIB* 637)

While these notes often draw on the language of love and care, they are nonetheless relentless in reminding teen girls that they cannot escape

God's watchful eye, as he searches for any hint of their disloyalty or non-compliance. Such microsurveillance by a controlling and all-seeing, all-knowing God is highly intimidating, denying *True Images* readers any sense of privacy and agency. It echoes the tactics used by coercive controllers to portray themselves as omniscient and omnipresent in their victims' lives. This, in turn, reinforces teen girl readers' need to constantly police their own behaviour, lest God spies them acting in a way that arouses his displeasure. They are given no choice about whether or not to accept this divine "love," and there seems to be no way that they can decline God's ever-presence in their lives.

Beyond these "Love Notes," other editorial additions in *True Images* likewise drive home to teen girls that they cannot escape God's microsurveillance. One "Dare to Believe" note warns readers bluntly, "Trying to sneak one past God? He's not fooled by your disguises or pretenses. So if you're hiding something from him—'fess up. And if you're holding something back from him—give it up" (*TIB* 423). Another "Genuine" note reminds girls that they have *no* private places or spaces free from God's watchful eye—even their knicker drawer is apparently not off-limits to the deity's ever-present scrutiny:

> What do you have stashed in the bottom drawer of your dresser or under your bed (besides some dirty clothes)? What things about yourself do you try to hide? What are your deepest, darkest secrets? While it's okay not to advertise your personal life to the outside world, it's not okay to try to hide it from God. It doesn't work. Your life is laid out to him to see in full view and living color regardless of whether anyone else knows. He knows all your secrets. You're completely transparent in his eyes.
>
> (*TIB* 816)

The rhetoric here is both intimidating and deeply voyeuristic. The *True Images* God stalks teen girls, invading their most private spaces, unearthing their secrets, and telling them that "it's not okay" to keep anything to themselves. Girls' lives are "completely transparent," exposed in "full view" to the divine male gaze without their consent or approval. Any attempt to hide from this microsurveillance simply "doesn't work." Resistance is futile, escape is impossible.

Conclusion

This was a difficult chapter to write. When I first started reading the *Revolve* and *True Images* Bibles I found myself feeling tired, stressed, and anxious. I would painstakingly study their pages for hours at a time, only to put them aside for a while, feeling a sense of dread at the thought of opening them up again. I initially didn't understand why these Bibles had this effect on me. At first, I put it down to the small font size of the print and my aging eyes, or all the other things that were worrying me at the time (I began looking at these Bibles just as COVID took over the world). But as time went on, I started to notice a pattern in the pages I was poring over with such care—a pattern of intimidation, denigration, threat, isolation, microsurveillance, love-bombing, and microregulation—all encoded in the innumerable editorial notes that *True Images* and *Revolve* readers were expected to absorb. To be honest, it's pretty hard to miss. Especially if you've experienced it yourself.

Coercive control is a malignant form of intimate partner violence. It drains victims of their personhood, knocks their legs from under them, and ties them even tighter to the person who is causing them so much harm. And yet framed in religious rhetoric, the tactics of coercive control are presented in *True Images* and *Revolve* as perfectly acceptable and divinely sanctioned patterns of gender relationships. Whether they intend to or not, these Bibles enable complementarian gender roles to flourish; they normalize teenage girls' abuse in the name of male privilege; and they micromanage girls' behaviour, compelling them to cede their agency and control to men and male deities. What is more, these Bibles weaponize Christianity's sacred scripture as a means of sustaining and sanctifying every reprehensible element of coercive control.

Teenage girls deserve better than this.

Notes

1 Not all evangelical Christians accept the complementarian doctrine; some adhere to a more egalitarian understanding of divinely ordained gender roles, which recognize biblical gender hierarchies as a less-than-ideal pattern for men and women to follow, and which focus more on mutual partnership and respect between husband and wife (see Marsden 2018).
2 For more information about the relationship between power, control, and IPV, see the work carried out by the Domestic Abuse Intervention Programs (DAIP) organization, including their now-iconic power and control wheel: https://www.theduluthmodel.org/wheels/.
3 Coercive control is highly gendered; women and girls are more likely to be victims, while men are its primary perpetrators. I acknowledge that boys, men, and non-binary people may also be victimized by a coercively controlling partner (who likewise may have any gender identity). But given that this chapter explores the controlling relationship between teenage girls and a

male deity, as portrayed in some teen girl Bibles, I typically refer to victims of coercive control as female and perpetrators as male. This in no way denies or downplays the experiences of coercive control victims who do not identify as women or girls.
4 The term "gaslighting" comes from the 1944 movie *Gaslight*, starring Charles Boyer and Ingrid Bergman. In essence, gaslighting involves the use of deception to manipulate and confuse another person by challenging their own memories or experiences and bombarding them with mixed messages to the point that they begin to question their own reality and sanity. As Fontes explains, "An abuser who gaslights his partner is trying to disorient her and make her seem crazy to herself and others, strengthening his control over her" (2015, 44). See also Hayes and Jeffries (2015, 37).
5 Klein notes that many Christian women in conservative evangelical communities believe that their sense of pride or achievement in their personal skills are sinful, because they contradict the gender expectations they have learned in both religious and secular contexts (2018 ch. 5, Kindle).
6 This is repeated almost verbatim in a *Revolve* "Daily Devos" note ,which tells girls that they will recognize Mr Right "*if* and when God sends him to you" (*RB* 305; emphasis added).
7 The *Bible for Teen Girls* does mention God's surveillance a few times, but it is framed far more benignly. It also acknowledges the problematic implications of this ever-present divine gaze, although reassures girls not to worry: "God knows more about you than you know about yourself. While being under the watchful gaze of the all-knowing God can sound spooky or worse, it's a good thing to be noticed by the Lord" (*BTG* 675).

Conclusion

A Bible marketed to teenage girls could be a pretty awesome thing. It could encourage its readers to think deeply about their emotional, spiritual, and relational wellbeing. It could offer them practical advice about how to navigate this ever-changing and complex world. It could empower teen girls to engage in advocacy on behalf of themselves, their communities, and the wider world. It could speak honestly but sensitively about the many challenges some teen girls face in their everyday lives: family problems and family violence, mental illness, learning difficulties, bullying, queer sexualities, sexism, racism, colourism, homophobia, transphobia, poverty, ableism, peer pressure, and all sorts of romantic relationship crises. Particularly, it could educate girls about gender-based violence in all its forms (including sexual harm, emotional abuse, and coercive control), offering them valuable advice around preventing it, reporting it, and healing from it. A teen girl Bible *could* invite its readers to contemplate and learn about all these things and more, through the multifaceted lens of their faith.

The teen girl Bibles I looked at in this book miss this valuable opportunity. While they touch on some of the issues mentioned above, they often do so within a particularly narrow (and often deeply unhelpful) framework. With their eye too firmly fixed on evangelical purity discourse and complementarian doctrine, they offer teen girls a narrative about themselves that is rooted in subordination and shame. They reinforce patriarchal gender norms that attempt to keep women "in their place." They consistently erase the existence of sexual harm and intimate partner violence (from the biblical texts and girls' own lives), reinforcing discourses that sustain the prevalence of these crimes, all the while exonerating perpetrators and blaming and stigmatizing their victims. Some of these Bibles even (wittingly or not) adopt tactics akin to those used in coercively controlling relationships, which serve to keep their teen girl readers silent, compliant, and subordinated. They present teen girls with an evangelical God who wants to terrorize them, control them, and dominate them, rather than see them flourish and thrive.

Given all the strong, smart, and inspiring teenage girls that I've met (my students, friends, and family members), I am pretty sure that many readers of *True Images*, *Revolve*, and the *Bible for Teen Girls* are more than capable of critiquing and dismissing these Bibles' harmful rhetoric. However, as Klein (2018) and Stanley (2020) both remind us, this rhetoric can have a hugely negative impact on many young women's lives, one that continues to haunt them far beyond their teenage years. And I strongly suspect that some teenage readers *will* be negatively impacted by the discourses articulated in these Bibles' incessant editorial additions.

If I could create an *alternative* teen girl Bible, then, what would it look like? Not pink, for a start. There wouldn't be a flower or a love heart in sight (not that there's anything wrong with flowers or love hearts, be they pink or otherwise). Instead, alongside the biblical text, I would include heaps of honest conversations about the Bible's various "texts of terror" that portray gendered violence in all its forms. I would offer teen girl readers the tools to read these texts "against the grain," so that they could learn to challenge and dismantle their often-harmful ideologies. I would also highlight biblical texts that speak so clearly and passionately about the divine imperative for social justice and the care of the most marginalized members of our society. I would offer a ton of information and advice that empowers teenage girls to make informed choices about their lives; to be advocates for their own and others' rights; to have the confidence to do amazing things in their communities; to navigate healthy sexual/romantic relationships and learn to recognize abusive and unhealthy relationships; to understand and navigate discourses of sexual consent; to take care of their mental wellbeing; to find support *as soon as* they need it; to use their voices to SPEAK OUT without shame; and, most importantly, to be *proud* of being a teenage girl. Because let's be honest, there's an awful lot to be proud of.

Bibliography

Bibles Referenced

Bible for Teen Girls. 2015. Grand Rapids, MI: Zondervan.
Revolution Bible for Teen Guys. 2017. Grand Rapids, MI: Zondervan.
Revolve Bible. 2012. Nashville, TN: Thomas Nelson.
Revolve: The Complete New Testament. 2003. Nashville, TN: Thomas Nelson.
True Images Bible for Teen Girls. 2017. Grand Rapids, MI: Zondervan.

Works Consulted

Allen, Louisa. 2005. "'Say Everything': Exploring Young People's Suggestions for Improving Sexuality Education." *Sex Education* 5 (4): 389–404. https://doi.org/10.1080/14681810500278493.

Allen, Louisa. 2013. "Girls' Portraits of Desire: Picturing a Missing Discourse." *Gender and Education* 25 (3): 295–310. https://doi.org/10.1080/09540253.2012.752795.

Anne, Libby. 2012. "How the Modesty Doctrine Fuels Rape Culture." *Patheos*, 10 December. https://www.patheos.com/blogs/lovejoyfeminism/2012/12/how-the-modesty-doctrine-fuels-rape-culture.html.

Beatly, Katelyn. 2019. "Joshua Harris and the Sexual Prosperity Gospel." *Religion News Service*, 26 July. www.religionnews.com/2019/07/26/joshua-harris-and-the-sexual-prosperity- gospel/.

Bennetch, Rebekah J. 2009. "The Gospel According to *Glamour*: A Rhetorical Analysis of Revolve: The Complete New Testament." Unpublished MA thesis, University of Saskatchewan, Saskatoon. https://core.ac.uk/reader/226123640.

Black, Edwin. 1993. "The Second Persona." In *Landmark Essays on Rhetorical Criticism*, edited by Thomas Benson, 161–172. Davis, CA: Hermagoras Press.

Blyth, Caroline. 2010. *The Narrative of Rape in Genesis 34: Interpreting Dinah's Silence*. Oxford: Oxford University Press, 2010.

Bibliography

Brenner, Athalya, and van Dijk-Hemmes, Fokkelien. 1993. *On Gendering Texts: Female and Male Voices in the Hebrew Bible*. Leiden: Brill.

Brownmiller, Susan. 1993. *Against Our Will: Men, Women, and Rape*. New York: Fawcett Books.

Burns, Catherine. 2005. *Sexual Violence and the Law in Japan*. Abingdon: RoutledgeCurzon.

Colgan, Emily J. 2018. "Let Him Romance You: Rape Culture and Gender Violence in Evangelical Christian Self-Help Literature." In *Rape Culture, Gender Violence, and Religion: Christian Perspectives*, edited by Caroline Blyth, Emily J. Colgan, and Katie B. Edwards, 9–26. New York: Palgrave Macmillan.

Collins, Patricia Hill. 2000. *Black Feminist Thought: Knowledge, Consciousness, and the Politics of Empowerment*. 2nd ed. New York: Routledge.

Colopy, Elsa Kok. 2012. *Pure Love, Pure Life: Exploring God's Heart on Purity*. Grand Rapids, MI: Zondervan.

Crown Prosecution Service. 2020. "Indecent and Prohibited Images of Children." https://www.cps.gov.uk/legal-guidance/indecent-and-prohibited-images-children.

Day, Linda. 1999. "Teaching the Prophetic Marriage Metaphor Texts." *Teaching Theology and Religion* 2 (3): 173–179. https://doi.org/10.1111/1467-9647.00059.

Day, Linda. 2000. "Rhetoric and Domestic Violence in Ezekiel 16." *Biblical Interpretation A Journal of Contemporary Approaches* 8 (3): 205–230. https://doi.org/10.1163/156851500750096327.

Department of Justice. (2020). "Citizens' Guide to U.S. Federal Law on Child Pornography," 28 May. https://www.justice.gov/criminal-ceos/citizens-guide-us-federal-law-child-pornography.

Domoney-Lyttle, Zanne. 2019. "Graphic Assault: Reading Sexual Assault and Rape Narratives in Biblical Comics." *The Bible and Critical Theory* 15 (2): 49–65. https://www.bibleandcriticaltheory.com/issues/vol-15-no-2-2019-bible-and-critical-theory/graphic-assault-reading-sexual-assault-and-rape-narratives-in-biblical-comics/.

Dunbar, Ericka S. 2019. "For Such a Time as This? #UsToo: Representations of Sexual Trafficking, Collective Trauma, and Horror in the Book of Esther." *The Bible and Critical Theory* 15 (2): 29–48. https://www.bibleandcriticaltheory.com/issues/vol-15-no-2-2019-bible-and-critical-theory/for-such-a-time-as-this-ustoo-representations-of-sexual-trafficking-collective-trauma-and-horror-in-the-book-of-esther/.

Duran, Nicole. 2003. "Who Wants to Marry a Persian King? Gender Games and Wars and the Book of Esther." In *Pregnant Passion: Gender, Sex and Violence in the Bible*, edited by Cheryl Kirk Duggan, 71–84. Atlanta: Society of Biblical Literature.

Edwards, Katie M., Jessica A. Turchik, Christina M. Dardis, Nicole Reynolds, and Christine A. Gidycz. 2011. "Rape Myths: History, Individual

and Institutional-Level Presence, and Implications for Change." *Sex Roles* 65: 761–773. https://doi.org/10.1007/s11199-011-9943-2.
Eldredge, John, and Stasi. 2005. *Captivating: Unveiling the Mystery of a Woman's Soul*. Nashville, TN: Thomas Nelson.
Ethridge, Stacey, and Stephen Arterburn. 2004. *Every Young Woman's Battle: Guarding Your Mind, Heart, and Body in a Sex-Saturated World*. Colorado Springs: WaterBrook Press.
Exum, J. Cheryl. 2016. *Fragmented Women: Feminist (Sub)versions of Biblical Narratives*. 2nd ed. London: Bloomsbury T&T Clark.
Fahs, Breanne. 2010. "Daddy's Little Girls: On the Perils of Chastity Clubs, Purity Balls and Ritualised Abstinence." *Frontiers* 31 (3): 116–142. https://www.muse.jhu.edu/article/402749.
Fitzgerald, Frances. 2017. *The Evangelicals: The Struggle to Shape America*. New York: Simon & Schuster.
Fontes, Lisa Aronson. 2015. *Invisible Chains: Overcoming Coercive Control in Your Intimate Relationship*. New York: Guilford Publications.
Fox, Michael V. 1991. *Character and Ideology in the Book of Esther*. 2nd ed. Grand Rapids, MI: Eerdmans.
Gilmore, Jane. 2019. *Fixed It: Violence and the Representation of Women in the Media*. Melbourne: Viking.
Gilmore, Jane. 2020. "Fixed It: Why Was He In Court?" *Jane Gilmore*. 7 May. https://janegilmore.com/fixedit-why-was-he-in-court-2/.
Gresh, Dannah. 2011. *Secret Keeper: The Delicate Power of Modesty*. 3rd ed. Chicago: Moody Publishers. Kindle.
Gresh, Dannah. 2012. *And the Bride Wore White: Seven Secrets to Sexual Purity*. Chicago: Moody Publishers. Kindle.
Harding, James. 2016. "Homophobia and Masculine Domination in Judges 19–21." *Bible and Critical Theory* 12 (2): 41–74. https://www.bibleandcriticaltheory.com/issues/vol12-no2-2016/vol-12-no-2-2016-homophobia-and-masculine-domination-in-judges-19-21/.
Hayes, Sharon, and Samantha Jeffries. 2015. *Romantic Terrorism: An Auto-Ethnography of Domestic Violence, Victimization and Survival*. London: Palgrave Pivot. https://doi-org.ezproxy.auckland.ac.nz/10.1057/9781137468499.
Hendershot, Heather. 2002. "Virgins for Jesus: The Gender Politics of Therapeutic Christian Fundamentalist Media." In *Hop on Pop: The Politics and Pleasures of Popular Culture*, edited by Henry Jenkins, Tara McPherson, and Jane Shattuc, 88–104. Durham: Duke University Press.
Hennessy, Don. 2012. *How He Gets into Her Head: The Mind of the Male Intimate Abuser*. Cork: Cork University Press.
Hill, Jess. 2019. *See What You Made Me Do: Power, Control and Domestic Abuse*. Melbourne: Black Inc.
hooks, bell. 1998. "Naked without Shame: A Counter-hegemonic Body Politic." In *Talking Visions: Multicultural Feminism in a Transnational Age*, edited by Ella Shohat, 65–73. Cambridge, MA: MIT Press.

Junior, Nyasha. 2019. *Reimagining Hagar: Blackness and Bible*. Oxford: Oxford University Press.

Kaell, Hilary. 2010. "Christian Teens and Biblezines: An Analysis of *Revolve, The Complete New Testament*." *Journal of Religion and Popular Culture* 22 (3): 1–17. https://doi.org/10.3138/jrpc.22.3.002.

Kirgiss, Crystal. 2011. *More than Skin Deep: A Guide to Self and Soul*. Grand Rapids, MI: Zondervan.

Klein, Linda Kay. 2018. *Pure: Inside the Evangelical Movement that Shaped a Generation of Young Women and How I Broke Free*. Atria Books. Kindle.

Klement, Kathryn R., and Brad J. Sagarin. 2017. "Nobody Wants to Date a Whore: Rape- Supportive Messages in Women-Directed Christian Dating Books." *Sexuality & Culture* 21, (2017): 205–223. https://doi.org/10.1007/s12119-016-9390-x.

Koon-Magnin, Sarah, and Corina Schulze. 2019. "Providing and Receiving Sexual Assault Disclosures: Findings From a Sexually Diverse Sample of Young Adults." *Journal of Interpersonal Violence* 34 (2): 416–441. https://doi.org/10.1177/0886260516641280.

Lebotwitz, Leslie, and Susan Roth. 1994. "'I Felt Like a Slut': The Cultural Context and Women's Response to Being Raped." *Journal of Traumatic Stress* 7: 363–390. https://doi.org/10.1007/BF02102783.

Liddell, Marg, and Anastasia Powell. 2015. "What's In a Name? Online Child Abuse Material Is Not 'Pornography'." *The Conversation*, 13 August. https://theconversation.com/whats-in-a-name-online-child-abuse-material-is-not-pornography-45840.

Magdalene, F. Rachel. 1995. Ancient Near Eastern Treaty-Curses and the Ultimate Texts of Terror: A Study of the Language of Divine Sexual Abuse in the Prophetic Corpus." In *A Feminist Companion to the Bible: The Latter Prophets*, edited by Athalya Brenner, 326–354. Sheffield: Sheffield Academic Press.

Marsden, Daphne. 2018. "The Church's Contribution to Domestic Violence: Submission, Headship, and Patriarchy." In *Rape Culture, Gender Violence, and Religion: Christian Perspectives*, edited by Caroline Blyth, Emily J. Colgan, and Katie B. Edwards, 73–95. New York: Palgrave Macmillan.

Martin, Bekah Hamrick. 2013. *The Bare Naked Truth*. Grand Rapids, MI: Zondervan.

Moslener, Sarah. 2015. *Virgin Nation: Sexual Purity and American Adolescence*. New York: Oxford University Press. Kindle.

Moslener, Sarah. 2017. "Material World: Gender and the Bible in Evangelical Purity Culture." In *The Bible and Feminism: Remapping the Field*, edited by Yvonne Sherwood, 608–621. Oxford: Oxford University Press.

Moughtin-Mumby, Sharon. 2008. *Sexual and Marital Metaphors in Hosea, Jeremiah, Isaiah, and Ezekiel*. Oxford: Oxford University Press.

Nason-Clark, Nancy. 1997. *The Battered Wife: How Christians Confront Family Violence*. Louisville, KY: Westminster John Knox.

Nason-Clark, Nancy. 1999. "Shattered Silence or Holy Hush: Emerging Definitions of Violence against Women." *Journal of Family Ministry* 13 (1): 39–56.

Nord, David Paul. 2004. *Faith in Reading: Religious Publication and the Birth of Mass Media*. Oxford: Oxford University Press.
Paynter, Helen. 2020. *Telling Terror in Judges 19: Rape and Reparation for the Levite's Wife*. Rape Culture, Religion, and the Bible. Abingdon: Routledge.
Pew Research Centre. 2019a. "Religious Landscape Study: Political Ideology." https://www.pewforum.org/religious-landscape-study/political-ideology/.
Pew Research Centre. 2019b. "Religious Landscape Study: Political Party Affiliation." https://www.pewforum.org/religious-landscape-study/party-affiliation/.
Pew Research Centre. 2019c. "Religious Landscape Study: Racial and Ethnic Composition." https://www.pewforum.org/religious-landscape-study/racial-and-ethnic-composition/.
Pillow, Wanda. 2004. *Unfit Subjects: Educational Policy and the Teen Mother*. New York: Routledge Falmer.
Rape Crisis. 2020. "Fight or Flight Response." https://rapecrisis.org.uk/get-help/looking-for-tools-to-help-you-cope/feelings/fight-or-flight-response/.
Santelli, John S., Leslie M. Kantor, Stephanie A. Grillo, Ilene S. Speizer, Laura D. Lindberg, Jennifer Heitel, Amy T. Schalet, Maureen E. Lyon, Amanda J. Mason-Jones, Terry McBovern, Craig J. Heck, Jennifer Rogers, and Mary A. Ott. 2017. "Abstinence-Only-Until-Marriage: An Updated Review of U.S. Policies and Programs and Their Impact." *Journal of Adolescent Health* 61 (3): 273–280. https://doi.org/10.1016/j.jadohealth.2017.05.031.
Scholz, Susanne. 2005. "'Back Then It Was Legal': The Epistemological Imbalance in Readings of Biblical and Ancient Near Eastern Rape Legislation." *The Bible and Critical Theory* 1 (4): 36.1–36.22. https://www.bibleandcriticaltheory.com/issues/vol1-no4/vol-1-no-4-2005-back-then-it-was-legal-the-epistemological-imbalance-in-readings-of-biblical-and-ancient-near-eastern-rape-legislation/.
Scholz, Susanne. 2010. *Sacred Witness: Rape in the Hebrew Bible*. Minneapolis: Fortress.
Smart, Carol. 1989. *Feminism and the Power of Law*. London: Routledge.
Stanley, Olivia. 2020. "A Personal Encounter with Purity Culture in an Evangelical Christian School." *Women's Studies Journal* 34 (1–2): 116–29.
Stark, Evan. 2007. *Coercive Control: How Men Entrap Women in Personal Life*. Oxford: Oxford University Press.
Stiebert, Johanna. 2019. *Rape Myths, The Bible, and #MeToo*. Rape Culture, Religion, and the Bible. Abingdon: Routledge.
Tamez, Elsa. 1986. "The Woman Who Complicated the History of Salvation." In *New Eyes for Reading: Biblical and Theological Reflections by Women from the Third World*, edited by John S. Pobee and Barbel von Wartenberg-Potter, 5–17. Geneva: World Council of Churches.
United Nations. 2006. *Ending Violence against Women: From Words to Action*. New York: United Nations.

Vagianos, Alanna. 2017. "Why These Women Are Tackling The 'Second Assault' Of Reporting Sexual Violence." *Huffington Post.* 25 October. https://www.huffpost.com/entry/why-these-women-are-tackling-the-second-assault-of-reporting-sexual-violence_n_59ef76fae4b0bf1f88363c04.

Valenti, Jessica. 2009. *The Purity Myth: How America's Obsession with Virginity is Hurting Young Women.* Berkeley: Seal Press.

Weems, Renita J. 1988. *Just a Sister Away: A Womanist Vision of Women's Relationships in the Bible.* San Diego: LuraMedia.

Weems, Renita J. 1995. *Battered Love: Marriage, Sex, and Violence in the Hebrew Prophets.* Minneapolis: Fortress.

Weider, Nicole. 2015. *Project Inspired: Tips and Tricks to Staying True to Who You Are.* Grand Rapids, MI: Zondervan.

Williams, Delores S. 1993. *Sisters in the Wilderness: The Challenge of Womanist God-Talk.* Maryknoll, NY: Orbis Books.

Williams, Jean Calterone. 2011. "Battling a 'Sex-Saturated Society': The Abstinence Movement and the Politics of Sex Education." *Sexualities* 14 (4): 416–443. https://doi.org/10.1177/1363460711406460.

Zeichmann, Christopher B. 2018. "A Centurion and His 'Lover': A Text of Queer Terror." *The Shiloh Project,* 29 January. https://www.shilohproject.blog/a-centurion-and-his-lover-a-text-of-queer-terror/.

Index of authors

Allen, L. 9n5, 30, 75
Anne, L. 13
Arterburn, S. 19, 21, 30n2, 31n8, 31n10, 31n11, 32n17

Beatly, K. 31n7
Bennetch, R. J. 2, 3, 9n8
Black, E. 3
Blyth, C. 20, 34, 65n5, 65n6
Brenner, A. 51
Brownmiller, S. 20
Burns, C. 34

Colgan, E. J. 51, 66n13
Collins, P. C. 14
Colopy, E. K. 24
Crown Prosecution Service. 66n20

Day, L. 51, 52
Department of Justice. 61
Domoney-Lyttle, Z. 2019. 36
Dunbar, E. S. 2019. 49, 50
Duran, N. 50

Edwards, K. M. 26, 41
Eldredge, J. 66n13
Eldredge, S. 66n13
Ethridge, S. 19, 21, 30n2, 31n8, 31n10, 31n11, 32n17
Exum, J. C. 65n7, 65n8

Fahs, B. 21, 22, 24, 25, 28, 29, 30, 30n2, 30n3, 31n6, 32n12, 33, 34
Fitzgerald, F. 8n1

Fontes, L. A. 71, 74, 84, 85, 86, 92, 96n4
Fox, M. V. 50

Gilmore, J. 54, 65n10, 65n11, 65n12
Gresh, D. 18, 19, 21, 22, 30n2, 31n7, 31n9, 31n10, 31n11, 32n12, 65n9

Harding, J. 65n7
Hayes, S. 69, 70, 71, 74, 75, 81, 84, 85, 96n4
Hendershot, H. 28, 34
Hennessy, D. 81
Hill, J. 72, 74, 81, 85, 92
Hooks, B. 32n16

Jeffries, S. 69, 70, 71, 74, 75, 81, 84, 85, 96n4
Junior, N. 65n3

Kaell, H. 2, 9n8
Kirgiss, C. 24
Klein, L. K. 1, 10, 11, 13, 14, 17, 18, 21, 22, 27, 31n6, 31n7, 32n13, 33, 64, 65, 69, 75, 96n5, 98
Klement, K. R. 3, 10, 12, 19, 25, 28, 30n2, 32n17
Koon-Magnin, S. 65

Lebotwitz, L. 20
Liddell, M. 67

Magdalene, F. R. 51
Marsden, D. 68, 69, 95n1

Index of authors

Martin, B. H. 15
Moslener, S. 1, 2, 3, 6, 8n1, 9n7, 9n8, 11, 12, 14, 19, 28, 30n1, 31n5
Moughtin-Mumby, S. 51

Nason-Clark, N. 69
Nord, D. P. 1

Paynter, H. 43, 65n7
Pew Research Centre. 1, 8n1, 8n2
Pillow, W. 25
Powell, A. 67

Rape Crisis. 66n18
Roth, S. 20

Sagarin, B. J. 3, 10, 12, 19, 25, 28, 30n2, 32n17
Santelli, J. S. 31n6
Scholz, S. 36, 51, 59, 65n5, 65n7, 65n8, 66n19
Schulze, C. 65
Smart, C. 33

Stanley, O. 3, 10, 13, 16, 21, 22, 26, 28, 30n2, 30n4, 32n12, 32n13, 75, 98
Stark, E. 70, 71, 72, 74, 84, 85, 86, 92
Stiebert, J. 58, 59, 65n1, 65n5, 66n19

Tamez, E. 36

United Nations. 69

Vagianos, A. 65
Valenti, J. 10, 13, 14, 16, 18, 25, 27, 28, 29, 30n3, 31n6, 32n16
van Dijk-Hemmes, F. 51

Weems, R. J. 36, 51, 52
Weider, N. 37
Williams, D. S. 36
Williams, J. C. 12, 31n6

Zeichmann, C. B. 66n16

Index of biblical citations

Hebrew Bible

Genesis 1:27 p.76
Genesis 2:3 p.89
Genesis 4 p.16
Genesis 12:2 p.35
Genesis 13:16 p.35
Genesis 16 pp.35-38, 58, 65n2
Genesis 17:5 p.65n2
Genesis 17:15 p.65n2
Genesis 19 pp.40, 58, 59, 66n15
Genesis 21 pp.35-36, 65n2, 65n4
Genesis 30 pp.38, 58
Genesis 34 pp.38-39, 58–9, 65n5
Genesis 35:22 p.59
Genesis 39 pp.39-42
Genesis 49:3-4 p.59
Exodus 31:12 p.89
Leviticus 19:20-22 p.58
Numbers 12 p.73
Numbers 25:6-8 p.58
Numbers 31:18 p.58
Deuteronomy 21:10-14 p.58
Deuteronomy 22:25-27 pp.59, 66n18
Deuteronomy 22:28-29 p.59
Deuteronomy 30:15-20 p.72
Judges 19-21 pp.40, 42–3, 58, 59, 65n7
2 Samuel 10:1-5 p.66n17
2 Samuel 11 pp.43-46
2 Samuel 13 pp.46-49
2 Samuel 15:13-16 p.59
2 Samuel 16:20-23 p.59
2 Samuel 20:3 p.59
Esther 1-2 pp.49-51
Psalms 2:11 p.74
Psalms 39:1 p.80
Proverbs 7:10 pp.24, 32n15
Ecclesiastes 12:13-14 p.73
Song of Songs 4:12 p.16
Isaiah 3:16-24 pp.57, 66n14
Isaiah 41:29 p.5
Isaiah 47:2-3 p.58
Jeremiah 2:1-4:4 pp.51, 52
Jeremiah 13:22 p.58
Jeremiah 38:23 p.58
Lamentations 1:8-10 p.58
Lamentations 5:11 p.58
Ezekiel 16 pp.51-53
Ezekiel 23 pp.51, 52
Hosea 1-3 pp.51, 53–7, 66n13
Zechariah 14:2 p.58

New Testament

Matthew 5:27-29 p.32n13
Matthew 8:5-13 pp.58, 66n16
Luke 7:1-10 pp.58, 66n16
John 8:2-11 p.19
Revelation 2:22 p.58
17 p.58

For Product Safety Concerns and Information please contact our EU representative GPSR@taylorandfrancis.com
Taylor & Francis Verlag GmbH, Kaufingerstraße 24, 80331 München, Germany